Streetwise Safety for Children

by
Michael DePasquale Jr.

Charles E. Tuttle Co., Inc.
Boston • Rutland, Vermont • Tokyo

First published in 1995 by Charles E. Tuttle Compnay, Inc. of
Rutland, Vermont, and Tokyo, Japan, with editorial offices at
153 Milk Street, Boston, Massachusetts 02109

Library of Congress Cataloging-in-Publication Data

DePasquale, Michael.
    Streetwise safety for children / by Michael DePasquale, Jr.
        p.   cm.   —(Streetwise safety series)
    ISBN 0–8048–3013–4
    1. Safety education. 2. Self-defense for children. 3. Children's acci-
dents—Prevention. I. Title. II. Series.
HQ770.7.D47 1995
613.6—dc20   94-46252
                                                                   CIP

Cover design by Fahrenheit

First edition

1 3 5 7 9 10 8 6 4 2

Printed in the United States of America

Disclaimer
Please note that the publisher of this instructional book is not responsible in
any manner whatsoever for any injury that may result from practicing the
techniques and/or following the instructions given within. Since the physical
activities described herein may be too strenuous in nature for some readers
to engage in safely, it is essential that a physician be consulted prior to
training.

This book is dedicated to my Mom and Dad who gave me a great life growing up, and cared about the safety of all of us. I also want to thank my Aunts, Uncles, and Grandparents for their concern on our behalf. I also want to dedicate this book to all the children around the world that they may always be safe, wherever they may go.

SPECIAL ACKNOWLEDGMENTS

Special thanks are due to my father, Michael DePasquale, Sr. for his knowledge and help in the crime prevention and self-defense areas. I would also like to thank my staff, who helped make this book possible, Melissa E. Kisla (Missy), Gail Miller, Dotty Pillischer, Monica Schulman, Eileen Muenchen, James Chin and Roger Chan. I would also like to thank James Kneisler for his photography, Mark Piano, Myron King and Ed Salter for art direction and illustration.

Models appearing in this book include: Bonnie & David Young, Noemi, Vincent, Vicente & Jose Manuel Lim, Kevin & Sue Bull, James P. & James P. II Kneisler, Anna (Cookie) and Mark Guterrez, Gregory Denis, and Jeff Walensky, and Lorie & Nicole Gregory.

A special thanks to "Crime Prevention Consultants and Security Experts," Bill D'Urso, Robert Suggs, Richard Dillon, Rick Fike, Michael DePasquale, Sr., and Tom Patire for their assistance.

GENERAL ACKNOWLEDGMENTS

It would be very difficult for us to identify all of the sources of the crime prevention and self-defense information used to create this book, but we would like to thank those departments, organizations and reference books that helped make this publication an actuality:

The New York City Police Department

United States Department of Justice

The Federal Bureau of Investigation

National Criminal of Justice Information and

Statistic Service

International Protection Inc.

Interdome Group Inc.

State of the Art Security

The Truth About Self Protection

How to Protect Yourself From Crime

How to Keep From Being Robbed Raped & Ripped Off

Total Self-Protection

CONTENTS

When one waits long enough, he is sure to receive what he waited for. This volume is the result of many years of contact with children, and is filled with information that is specifically geared to children of all ages. Additionally, it addresses safety problems in a way that will interest parents, thus generating a desire to understand the various problems facing children today. Throughout the book we find ourselves emotionally experiencing each problem and viewing children's daily lives in a far different manner.

Each chapter is loaded with important commentary and advice, which, if followed, will shield children against the everyday dangers of kidnapping and assault—to name a few problems. The clear manner in which the author explains each problem and how to prepare for it is what makes this a most unusual volume. Problems that may arise when leaving a child home alone are discussed with clarity from a professional's outlook, which provides the reader with a wealth of knowledge for coping with any situation that comes about. Problem areas faced by children are described in a lucid manner, followed by advice and suggestions relative to preparation and defense against any intrusion. Virtually every imaginable safety area is covered. One of the most vulnerable parts of any child's day is the time he or she spends traveling between home and school. Every day, children must make their way through a myriad of traveling situations throughout which they must be aware of where they are, where they are going, and the people around them.

The author has cleverly taken problem situations and shows how to first protect against intrusion, then defend against any breach. This makes *Streetwise Safety for Children* a valuable asset to any parent. Indeed, I would recommend it to anyone in any profession. It has value to parents, older children (capable of reading it), security personnel, teachers, school bus drivers, and others engaged in transporting or teaching children. For parents it becomes a training manual with full coverage of any potential danger to their children. Each chapter is fully explained with emphasis placed on specific situations. At no place in this book is there a situation or condition that is not covered from beginning to end. Such subjects as lighting, locks, telephones, and alarm systems are described in a manner that the uninitiated should digest with ease.

Mr. DePasquale comes well equipped to write this book. He is internationally known and recognized as a fine instructor with over 30 years of experience in martial arts. He has instructed peace officers throughout the United States as well as in Canada, Italy and Mexico. He holds a martial arts rank of Nidai Shihan in Yoshitsune Waza Ju-Jitsu. He has been the subject of articles in newspapers, magazines, college periodicals and organization periodicals. He has also appeared in nine martial arts motion pictures made both here in the U.S. as well as in the Orient. In addition he has appeared on numerous television and radio shows, such as "Regis Philbin," "Yo MTV Raps," "Nickelodeon," "Attitudes" and network news, speaking about F.U.M.A.'S streetwise safety and self-defense techniques and seminars.

Experience as a security officer has afforded him a "hands-on" opportunity to work as a bodyguard, executive security engineer and protection consultant. I cannot recommend this volume more highly. The reader will find that it offers simple, down to the point solutions to serious problems.

BY MICHAEL DEPASQUALE SR.
Dai Shihan Yoshitsune Ju Jitsu
United States Army Criminal Investigation Division
Polygraphist
Retired Railroad Police
State Licensed Private Detective
Founder International Protection Systems Inc.
Lecturer, Terrorism And Explosives
US Government Security Agent

Streetwise Safety for Children

by Robert C. Suggs, Ph.D.
FUMA Crusade Against Crime Coordinator

Groups of high school students lie in wait for students of Elementary School X, at bus stops and along walking routes, attempting to sell the children drugs and threatening them if they do not make purchases. A couple of determined little girls turn the dealers over to police and then live in fear of retaliation for weeks.

A "cool" youth tall, well-dressed, and a role model in his own mind, attends Elementary School Y. In his school bag he carries a knife, to awe his school mates; a couple of condoms, to hand out to friends; and a wine cooler for lunch, to help reduce the terrible anguish imposed by mental challenge. A year later, before finishing 6th grade, he has been incarcerated for a lengthy term on assault and battery, but his place has been taken by imitators.

In a fight over turf between drug dealers at an *upper-middle class* high school, students bring guns to school in preparation for a shoot-out. A youth sees a fellow student hide a gun in his locker; he is threatened with death if he reports the presence of the weapon, but does so anyway. Although the threat is never carried out, he and his parents remain fearful for his life.

Drug dealers at a suburban high school dress ostentatiously in expensive preppy clothing, attend rock concerts and "raves," drive good cars, and openly brag about the amounts of money they make in their business, despite the constant presence of police patrols, who appear totally ignorant of their activities.

A well-known high school football star is arrested for the armed robbery of a group of friends in a local fast food establishment. For the school administration the only important question raised by his act is: should he be allowed to play in the first game of the season?

A group of upper middle class teenagers get drunk on New Year's Eve and decide to "torch" the local high school, causing $3 million in damages and resulting in the suspension of all school operations for over a year. One parent claims that this act was a legitimate free-speech protest against a "repressive" school regime — which failed to provide an indoor smoking area for the arsonists!

Members of a ring of elderly homosexual child abusers and pornographers — linked regional- and national by E-mail—hang out at shopping malls attracting young men with promises of gifts and money. They are apprehended and convicted, but refuse to divulge the fate of one of their victims, who has disappeared without a trace.

A class of 4th and 5th grade karate students is being briefed on a serial rapist known by police to be operating in the vicinity of their school. The instructor finishes his presentation, and students' hands begin to go up. Within a few minutes, 4 out of 5 of the girls in the class have told their classmates of male relatives and family "friends" — sexual predators — who their parents have warned them to avoid!

In an anti-abuse training session, a martial arts instructor gives suggestions on how to cope with threatening adult behaviors. From the back row comes the plaintive question: "What do you do when the person bothering you is your father?"

THE SITUATION

These few relatively commonplace examples from only one person's experience and knowledge illustrate the increasingly vicious world surrounding a large percentage of American children today, and the apparent inability of authorities to cope with this situation. The schools, the streets, the shopping malls, and even the once sacrosanct home, abound with threats to our nation's most important resource — our children. Law enforcement seems to be blind, or hobbled by courts, and standards of right and wrong seem infinitely negotiable. There is no indication that this world is going to miraculously change for the better at any time soon!

CRIME STATISTICS

Examples similar to those above, and worse, are everywhere. The real magnitude of the problem is unfortunately quite difficult to estimate, because of numerous problems with crime statistics produced by government, academic, and advocacy groups. These problems result to a large degree from inaccurate or incomplete reporting. It is estimated, for example, that 46% of all violent crimes, 44% of all rapes, and 36% of all crimes are never reported (and these estimates may not be valid either!). Further, there are differences between the ways that states define and report various kinds of crimes that make them difficult to summarize. There is also a tendency not to collect data on crimes committed by members of lower age groups (e.g., below age 12), in which children and youths are victims or perpetrators. There is also the lamentable tendency for all federal statistics to be intentionally altered to support requests for increased departmental funding, or to support the political agenda of political parties or administrations. This tendency is matched by non-government advocacy groups' practices of grossly exaggerating the frequency of certain types of crimes to justify their own existence as advocates. Data on missing children, for example, gives the impression that these children are all victims of unknown kidnappers, when, in fact, many have gone willingly with family members fighting custody battles in increasingly capricious courts, or are voluntary runaways. Statistics summarized at national, state, or local levels also blur significant differences in types and frequencies of crimes between states or cities and their suburbs.

Finally, while over 50% of reported cases of child abuse cannot be substantiated, there is also anecdotal evidence of an opposing tendency for some of the worst kinds of child abuse to be underreported; for example sexual abuse of children, which often involves family members and carries a high degree of public disapproval. In such areas, statistics may show only the tip of the iceberg due to reluctance of children to report such crimes and the unwillingness of child advocates to run the risk of serious legal retaliation by defendants if complaints of abuse cannot be fully substantiated.

THE PREVALENCE OF CRIME

Let's examine some of the more reliable information available from various sources, to sketch the dimensions of the problem of child safety.

FAMILY VIOLENCE

Figures show that the American family is increasingly violent: offenders tend to come from within the family and circle of acquaintances of the victim, and the predominant causes seems to be domestic disputes or arguments.

CHILDREN AND CRIME: Victims and Perpetrators

The late teen-age component of society is also becoming increasingly active in crime. For example, FBI data shows that persons between the ages of 15 and 24 account for an unusually high number of arrests for auto thefts, arson, and driving under the influence of alcohol. United States Department of Justice (USDOJ) tables show that murder per 100,000 teenagers has risen dramatically in the 14-18 year age group. They further show that children under age 17 are victims of nearly a quarter of the murders committed by these youths. More than 75% of all juvenile homicides in the US were committed with guns, and 33% of the murder victims killed by guns were under 19 years of age. In the minority communities, the situation is much worse: gunshot wounds are the leading cause of death among black youth. Nearly two thirds of all rapes were committed against girls 17 years old or younger, and about one third take place in the victim's own home.

CRIME IN SCHOOLS

In school, the situation is likewise hazardous: USDOJ tables show that about 9% of all students report either being physically victimized or having their property destroyed at school. The tables also report the easy availability of alcohol and marijuana at a large percentage of schools, as well as the presence of gangs in a sizable percentage of schools. While gangs are most frequently reported by lower income children in urban or suburban areas, there is also a significant amount of gang activity reported by students from higher income families and students in rural schools—old socio-economic and geographical stereotypes are breaking down! USDOJ tables show that many students, particularly either at school or on the way to school, again, particularly the younger students, are most vulnerable.

ABUSE AMONG CHILDREN

The early onset of alcohol and drug abuse among children is clearly documented. A surprising number of children took their first drinks or had their first experience with narcotics before age 10. It is noteworthy that alcohol and drug use occurs mainly at home or in the home of a friend, but 2% of the older students (i.e., those in 9th grade and up) also report using drugs or alcohol in school.

CHILD ABUSE

Data collection on child abuse compiled by the National Center of Child Abuse and Neglect (NCCAN) since 1976 shows a significant increase in rate of reporting of 331%. About 54% of these reports cannot be substantiated by investigation, but that does not mean they did not occur: nor does it mean that the substantiated cases represent all the cases of child abuse. Many remain unreported. Even with only 41% substantiated or "indicated" (i.e., there is good reason to suspect that abuse occurred) 993,000 children suffered abuse of one type or another during 1992, the last year for which we have data. While the largest number of victims suffered general neglect, 37% suffered physical or sexual abuse. Seventy-nine percent of all victims were least able to defend themselves, ie., they were 7 years old or younger and slightly over half were female. The perpetrators were in most cases (91%) parents and relatives, but "noncare-takers," foster parents, and facility and child care staff accounted for 7% of the cases.

PARENTAL RESPONSIBILITY FOR ACTION

What can children and parents do in this bleak situation? Plenty!!!

The major responsibility for protecting children resides with the parents and the parents alone. It is a sacred responsibility that can never be delegated to local schools, churches, or other organizations.

First, one must face up to one's own home situation, and recognize and objectively confront and surmount any problems that may exist there. Often, child abuse or evidence of other criminal or deviant behavior is tolerated in the home.

Next, parents must take a serious look at the total environment in which their children exist, assess the threats that exist there, persons, places, groups, and behaviors—begin to systematically warn children of these threats, and give them ways of avoiding them.

Although children can do little to defend themselves physically against older children or adults, when they are made aware of the dangers and the potential consequences of deviant behavior, no matter how "cool" that may seem, they can intelligently avoid the dangerous persons, places, and situations. It is precisely in this critical area of awareness-building that the parent is best equipped to function. This is no one-time, five-minute task, however. It requires constant awareness and attention to local developments, reading crime reports in local newspapers, watching local TV, keeping abreast of neighborhood gossip and activities, and encouraging close frank exchanges of information with your children. It also requires firmness and perseverance on the part of the parent, in order to be convincing to the child.

This book, the product of long and detailed research and experience in self-defense and crime awareness, provides a wealth of detailed information for concerned parents to develop their children's awareness to the many threats lurking behind often attractive forms. It may seem a shame to remove the innocence of childhood by talking to children about the grim realities of a world that has gone tragically wrong, but make no mistake about it, the kid drug dealer, the pervert, the rapist, the teenage gang member and their like will not hesitate one nanosecond to remove your children's innocence—FOREVER.

As the old saying goes, forewarned is forearmed, and this excellent work will enable you to adequately arm your children against the threats that they may encounter in the jungles of 20th century America.

• Dr. Robert C. Suggs received his B.A., M.A., and Ph.D. degrees in anthropology from Columbia University, and is an authority on the cultures and prehistory of Polynesia. A fifth degree black belt in Tang Soo Do karate, he is the International Coordinator for the Federation of United Martial Artists (FUMA), and the FUMA columnist for *Karate International Magazine*. He served in both the USMC and the USN in enlisted areas. He is the author of numerous books and articles on anthropology and Soviet Military affairs, and a professional translator of works on these subjects in several European languages.

Potential Danger in Your Home Environment

HOME SECURITY

Many crimes committed in the home could be avoided with proper precautions. You need to systematically check all potentially vulnerable areas of your home environment on a daily basis.

Most of us would like to think crime won't happen to us. And, naturally, it is impossible to predict where and when a crime will occur. But there is much you and your family can do to create a safer home environment.

Coming home to find your house or apartment has been robbed is bad enough. Being there when someone is trying to rob it, or interfering, can be much worse.

The following safety tips will help you become more aware of and responsible about home security, and are practices you can teach your children.

LOCKS

It is practically impossible to prevent a criminal from entering your house through an outside door if the criminal has the determination, skills and the time to do so. Remember, a criminal wants to spend the least amount of time and effort in the illegal act as possible. Making it difficult for him to enter is often enough to deter him and send him on his way to an easier target. Sometimes all you need is the proper type of door and window locks.

DOORS

Lock your doors at all times. Each door to your home should have a peephole or wide angle viewer. If you have a small child, place a step stool next to the door. This way your child can also see who is at the door before letting anyone in.

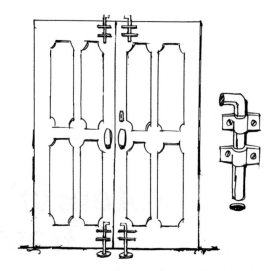

A solid wooden door or a hollow metal door snugly fit in its frame is most effective for safety, especially when secured with dead-bolt locks and double cylinder locks. A dead-bolt is superior to most other locks because it cannot be forced open with a knife, spatula, or similar tool. If the dead-bolt is sufficiently long, 1½ inches or more, the door becomes nearly impossible to pry open. Install a dead-lock on each outside door to supplement whatever locking devices you are presently using.

A double-cylinder lock is especially useful for doors with glass or wooden panels. This lock requires a key from both the outside and inside, thus preventing an intruder from reaching through broken glass or a broken panel to unlock the door from the inside. However, heed a word of caution about double-cylinder locks: In the event of a fire or a similar emergency, double-cylinder locks can delay occupants from exiting the house. Therefore, a key to the inside lock must always be readily at hand, and always within reach of your child.

WINDOWS

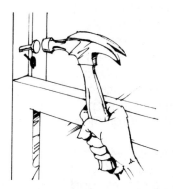
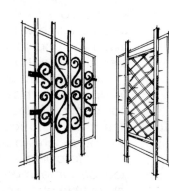

All windows of your home should have locks. Key locks work best. Further, you can use break-resistant glass to increase the security of your windows. Examine the windows in your home to determine how effective their locks are. If you find vulnerable windows, you may need special locks to secure your home. Check with a security specialist or with your local police department for helpful suggestions. An effective and simple way to secure your windows is to drill a slanted hole through the bottom window frame, or sash, halfway through the top frame (do not drill completely through the outside frame) and insert a metal pin or nail. This will prevent the window from being opened from the outside.

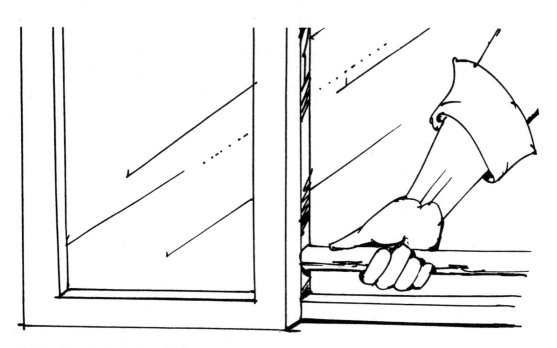

SLIDING GLASS DOORS

Sliding doors can be pried open easily unless you secure them. A steel rod or length of wood placed in the lower door track will prevent these doors from being opened. Also, a few screws drilled into the upper door track keep the door from being lifted off and out of its tracks by an intruder.

LIGHTING YOUR HOME

Denying a possible intruder the cover of darkness is a principal advantage of home lighting. A criminal is not likely to force his way into your home if his actions are highly visible. Most homes have lights positioned at their entrances. Turn many lights on, especially if your children will be home alone. Create the image of having many people home.

When you go to bed at night, do not turn off all the lights inside your house. Leave a front-room light on all night. If an intruder can see from the street that your exterior and interior lights are on, he will seek out a place that is poorly lit, rather than attempt to gain entry at the risk of being observed.

ALARMS

There are many home and business security systems available today. To decide what's right for you determine the value of what you wish to protect. Before you purchase an alarm system make sure that your child is able to arm and disarm it. I suggest you shop around with your child, before making your choice. Remember, an alarm signals only when an intruder is entering or exiting your home. If your property is properly secured, the intruder may not be able to enter in the first place.

THERE ARE THREE BASIC ALARM SYSTEMS:

1. Local: Designed to alert persons inside a home or office that someone is breaking in. These alarms generally frighten off intruders while alerting those present of possible danger.

2. Central or Remote: Designed to transmit signals to local police or security personnel. The police or security personnel will then investigate the alarm.
3: Proprietary: Designed to alarm a security force already in place within the location of the alarm. These systems are often used by warehouse or apartment complexes, providing security to property and residents.

REPORTING

Many crimes could be prevented if people would phone the police at the first sign of suspicious activity. Time is important, so report the crime or activity immediately.

Provide the police with all pertinent information: the address of the suspicious activity, the nature of it, and a complete description of any suspects or vehicles used. If reporting a crime, remember to provide police with your name, address and phone number.

Your child needs to know that it is O.K. to tell on someone. Most young children are intimidated by older children or adults, and may feel that it is not their place to say anything. It's your job as the parent to educate your children about safety. Role-play different situations with them. Thus they will come to feel secure in telling you of something suspicious, and they will have practiced what to do.

Remember that the information you provide to children needs to be simple and concrete. You need to foster a sense of trust and security in them, so they know they can always count on coming to you with anything.

STRANGERS

The following section is written so you can read it to your children and role-play scenarios with them. It is written in a tone they'll relate to and understand.

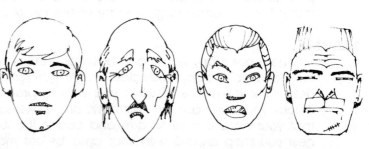

Explaining what you mean by "Stranger" is a good beginning to safety training. Children need to be advised (and often reminded) of the "Stranger-Danger" rule.

A stranger is someone you don't know. It can be a man or a woman, and old or young person. He or she doesn't have to look scary, ugly or mean. A stranger can be well-dressed, kind and very friendly. Anyone you haven't seen before, or who has not been introduced to you by a reliable adult or your parents, is a stranger. A stranger has many tricks to try to get to you like offering you candy or money.

Here are just a few tricks to be aware of: (PARENTS: These are great role-playing situations to practice safety):

1. Someone asks you to try and help him find his puppy. He has a picture of a puppy, a leash and a collar. What do you do? Tell him you hope he finds his puppy and run to a grown-up you know.
2. Someone drives up to you and asks for directions. Stay away from the car, stay out of reach, and walk/run the opposite way, or into a group of people.
3. Someone tries to bribe you with a pill or some form of drug. She promises you that you are going to feel like you're on a rollercoaster ride or just feel really good. Yell "No!" and run toward an adult you know.
4. Someone asks you if you want to earn money by carrying some packages to his car. Never go near strangers, and especially NEVER, NEVER follow someone you don't know to his car.
5. Be wary of anyone who is not in a full uniform posing as a police officer or fire fighter. Whatever they tell you, don't listen to them, and above all don't go with them. They may tell you that there has been an accident and your mommy has been hurt, or that your house is on fire and they were told to come get you. No matter what he or she may have to say, DO NOT GO WITH THEM. A real police officer, or fire fighter will always be in full uniform.

You and your parents should create an emergency system, or code word to be used in an emergency. Maybe a favorite word or flavor of ice-cream. This way if someone comes up to you, and there has been an emergency, he or she needs to say: "I'm here to get you, and the code word is _____," before you agree to go. This way you know that it is safe to go with that person.

SUSPICIOUS ACTIVITY

Suspicious activity can include a lot of behaviors that is not considered normal by most standards. Some are obvious, some more subtle and less detectable, yet all should be considered and reported. Here are some examples of suspicious activity:

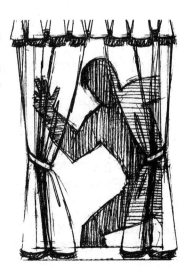

1. An unfamiliar vehicle repeatedly driving through your neighborhood, or one that stops and offers rides to children.
2. Anyone attempting to hide behind objects.
3. Someone sitting in an unfamiliar parked car observing a home or residents.
4. Furniture being loaded into a van when you are in doubt about the home occupants being present.
5. A person peeking in windows.

6. A person running from a home.
7. A person screaming.
8. Someone attempting to gain access to a home or car using force.

KIDNAPPING

Preventing kidnapping is an ongoing process of inspection, observation and implementation. Concern about kidnapping should be a constant mental and physical program with one objective in mind, to foil any attempt by a person who has the intent of taking your child.

Constantly repeat safety instructions to your children. Teach them to keep doors closed and locked when alone and to never open the door to a stranger. Thoroughly impress upon them that you expect them to follow your instructions to the letter. Try not to scare them, but let your children know kidnapping happens. Perhaps you can discuss a news story with them.

According to the U.S. Department of Justice report, "Missing, Abducted, Runaway, and Thrownaway Children in America" an estimated 3,200 to 4,600 non-family abductions were known to law enforcement in 1988. This estimate may even be low, due to the fact that some abductions may never be reported to the police because the victims of these assaults or rapes are ashamed or intimidated. The majority of children were abducted from the street, over 85% of them by force. Teenagers and girls were the most common victims. Two-thirds or more of the kidnappings involved sexual assault.

Children often fear not obeying and thus aggravating adults merely because they are adults. On the one hand we teach children to be respectful to adults and on the other hand we tell them not to obey all of them. To a young innocent mind this creates confusion. Thus the child, not wishing to aggravate parents, teachers or the police, follows the suggestions and demands of a stranger. You have to explain to your children that not all grown-ups are nice, that they need to be wary and trust their instincts. This facet of kidnapping prevention is absolutely the most important part of any program.

Family abduction occurs when a family member takes a child in violation of a custody agreement, or fails to return a child at the end of an agreed upon visit. The incidence of family abduction in 1988, according to the U.S. Department of Justice, was estimated at 354,100. The most common times for family abductions were in January and August, with episodes lasting from 2 days to a week, some lasting up to a month or more. Divorce is so prevalent today that a large percentage of children spend some portion of the year away from the parent they live with, visiting the other parent. If you're in this situation, teach your children to call you often especially if "plans" change.

FAMILY SECURITY PROCEDURES

The key to family security lies in participation. All family members should help by discussing each other's lifestyles to point out potential vulnerabilities. For example, a teenage boy with a late night job should let his family know his schedule.

One family member may have insight into another's potential threats. By opening the conversation to all family members, including children, a greater variety of topics can be discussed, and an attitude of group participation is encouraged. Develop a family security checklist, and get everyone involved. At the end of this chapter you will find a suggested checklist for home security.

LATCHKEY KIDS

Today nearly 42% of all American children between the ages of 5 and 9 are left home alone often, or at least occasionally. For older children this figure rises to 77%. The latchkey kid is a necessary evil of today's society. Before you decide to leave your child at home, there are a few factors you need to address.

1. Can your child lock and unlock the door? Can he/she turn on/off the alarm system? Does he/she know how to answer the door in your absence?
2. Can your child answer/dial the telephone? Is he/she able to operate the answering machine? Is he/she able to "field" phone calls so as not to let a caller know that you're not home? He/she could say you're in the bathroom, for instance.
3. Can your child tell time and read?
4. Can your child ABSOLUTELY reach you in case of an emergency?

You and your child must feel confident about his/her abilities to be left home alone. Ask your child how he/she feels about being home alone. If he/she shows any reluctance to the situation, he/she is not ready to be left alone.

Make sure you reassess the home alone situation periodically. Always keep the lines of communication open with your child. Your child needs to know that you are always there to alleviate his/her fears and concerns. If your child is no longer comfortable with the situation, try to make other arrangements. Some children feel that the opportunity to be left alone is a sign of greater responsibility, and thus feel more independent and capable. Other children become withdrawn and frightened, seeing the situation as one of abandonment. Don't forget what it feels like to be afraid. Those random noises that happen in the house can still startle even you sometimes. They can be terrifying to children, who may think there is a great big green monster with three heads and breathing fire, waiting to eat them when they walk through the kitchen door.

You must foster the feeling of safety in your latchkey child. An inflexible set of guidelines must be set-up before your child is left home alone. Remember, bored and restless children are sometimes drawn to destructive or delinquent behavior, so a strict set of guidelines needs to be designed and followed. Below you will find a sample set of guidelines which you can use as a beginning:

1. Start with a strict phone-in policy. Your child should call you (or some other trusted adult) as soon as he/she gets home from school.
2. Teach your children how to answer the phone, and to never let it be known that they are home alone. "My mother can't come to the phone right now, she's in the shower. Please give me your number, and she'll call you later."
3. Teach your children how to answer the door. There should be a list of who he/she is allowed to let in.
4. Develop a fire-escape plan and practice it!
5. Teach basic first-aid techniques.
6. Teach you children how to use kitchen appliances and the phone answering machine.
7. Have an emergency kit within reach. This kit should have all of the following, plus anything else you feel is necessary.
   • *Important phone numbers*
   • *Money*
   • *Basic first-aid kit*

THE TELEPHONE

Believe it or not, the telephone represents a serious vulnerable spot in your home security. Although originally designed as an innocent instrument of communication, the telephone is often used as an instrument of crime. By using the telephone, a person can have access to vital information you wouldn't normally disclose. Anyone who is persuasive, friendly and tactful can get you or your child to divulge private information.

Teach your children to never reveal that they are alone.

Teach them to never tell strangers their name, number or address. If the caller persists, tell children to hang up. Under no circumstances should they ever provide family information.

As a precautionary measure, exchange telephone numbers with a neighbor you can trust, in case of an emergency. It is also a good idea to have emergency numbers taped to your phone, so you and your children don't have to search for them in the event of a crisis.

Finally, hang up on all obscene or prank callers immediately, and report the call to the police and phone company. If such calls persist, do not engage in any type of conversation with the caller. Instead, inform authorities of the calls; they might wish to trace them.

STRANGERS AT THE DOOR

Don't admit anyone into your home unless they are familiar to you. A stranger's identity must be verified first. A peephole or viewer will help you by allowing you to see the stranger while he is still outside. You might also want to consider installing an intercom. This will allow you to speak with visitors without admitting them. If your home or apartment is equipped with a buzzer to admit callers, use it with discrimination. You or your child should never admit someone sight-unseen.

Assume the caller is falsifying his identity. Make sure at least one piece of ID has a picture of the caller. This also applies to police personnel. If a man calls, asking to read your meter, make him wait outside while you call his employer to verify the reading. If you have a door viewer and an intercom system, all of these precautions can be taken while the caller is still safely locked outside. If your children are home alone, teach them to not let anyone they don't know in under any circumstances. Teach them to dial 911 or the police if a stranger persists at the door.

A DOG

Throughout civilized history, dogs have been used to guard lives, property, locate criminals, contraband or children.

Although not all dogs will actually attack an intruder, the psychological advantage they provide is invaluable. Very few intruders will attempt a crime once they are aware of a dog's presence. A dog in the home, or outside, guarding the property, will help prevent intrusion.

NEIGHBORHOOD WATCH

One of the most effective methods of crime prevention is a simple, common-sense approach. Police can't be everywhere at all times. Half of all home burglaries and many child abductions occur during the day when alert neighbors could spot suspicious activity and report it. In many communities, concerned citizens are involved in a neighborhood watch, block watch, or citizen crime watch. The common goal of these groups is simple: neighbors watching out for one another. Check with the local police to see if your community has such a program. If so, join it. If not, why not start one?

HOME SECURITY CHECKLIST

A. SAFETY TIPS FOR YOU AND YOUR CHILDREN WHEN YOU'RE HOME:

1. Always keep all doors locked.
2. Know who is at the door before opening it.
3. If a stranger is persistent on the phone, do not reveal you are alone. Hang up.
4. Call the police if you hear noises outside the house.

B. INSTRUCTIONS TO LEAVE FOR A BABYSITTER:

1. Do not let friends visit.
2. Here are important phone numbers:
    a) Where I can be reached
    b) Children's doctor
    c) Fire
    d) Poison control center
3. Never reveal that adults are not at home.
4. Call police if you hear noises around the house.
5. Keep doors and lower-level windows locked at night.
6. If a stranger calls on the phone, hang up immediately. If he/she calls again contact the police and me.
7. Use extreme judgement when opening doors. Don't let anyone in unless you know him/her. If it's a friend of yours tell him/her you're not allowed to have company while babysitting.

C. STRANGERS (UTILITY WORKERS OR SERVICE EMPLOYEES) ENTER YOUR HOME:

1. Check the business identification of the person. If it's the electric or phone company or a cleaning service, he/she should have a photo i.d. Call the company before letting him/her in if you have any doubt.
2. Do not leave valuables in sight.
3. If possible, have someone there with you to greet the stranger.
    Note: If you live alone and you need the help of a maintenance person, of course you need to let them in! But only after you've checked their I.D. and called their company to verify them—then you should be ok.

D. GENERAL TIPS FOR HOME SECURITY:

1. If you and your child walk in on a burglar, do not fight him. Do as you are told and report the incident as soon as possible.
2. Make arrangements with your neighbors to keep an eye on each other. If a stranger is at your door, your neighbor can keep him/her under observation. If he/she breaks in, your neighbor can call the police.
3. Be certain that all outside doors are protected by a proper locking device. Deadbolt locks are best. Doors should be of solid construction and should fit snugly in their frames.
4. All windows should be properly protected by a window lock. Added security can be obtained by the use of a nail in a pre-drilled hole.
5. Do not leave keys in a hiding place. Burglars always look around for "hidden" keys before attempting to break in. Any hidden place you think of has been used before, and a professional criminal knows it!
6. Basement windows should be protected by bars or with heavy plastic sheeting.

7. Install a "peephole" in all outside doors. Intercoms are helpful for an added sense of security.

8. Dogs are a deterrent to any would-be intruder. If you have an attack dog be sure that you and your child train it well and that it remains under complete control at all times. A loose attack dog can hurt innocent people.

9. Police recommend marking all your appliances with an electric scriber on hidden locations (for future ID). Marking your child's toys, recreational equipment and bicycle is also recommended. Some police departments give decals for windows stating that the premises have been scribed.

10. If you and/or your child find that your home has been broken into, remember to leave everything alone and report the burglary to the police. The thief may have left fingerprints behind that could lead to an arrest.

11. Have alarms installed by reputable dealers. Units must be properly placed and controlled.

12. Always have keys ready to open doors, especially when arriving home late.

13. Keep outside lights on a timer so that the entrance to your home is always well illuminated.

14. Keep night chains on doors for added protection.

15. Secure any glass in the immediate vicinity of door knobs, and lock doors.

16. If you lose your keys, replace your locks immediately.

17. Do not reveal personal information to strangers on the phone.

18. Hedges, shrubs, fences and trees should not block visibility from street to windows.

19. Light the exterior of houses very well, and on all sides.

20. Light all gates and fences surrounding your property.

21. Illuminate all shadowed areas caused by trees, shrubbery or the house, especially around doors and windows.

E. GENERAL TIPS FOR APARTMENT DWELLERS' SECURITY:

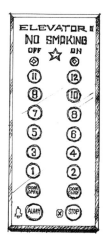

1. When moving into an apartment, look for these security features:
   a. Doormen or security guards to screen visitors.
   b. Attended elevators.
   c. Properly secured interior and exterior fire stairwells.
   d. Properly secured garages.
   e. Remotely operated door-opening systems, with intercom systems and closed-circuit T.V.
   f. Interior-view mirrors in self-secured elevators.
   g. Adequate lighting.
   h. Protection against alcoves or other blind spots being used as hiding places.
   i. Roof doors operable only from inside.

2. Change locks immediately after moving into your apartment.

3. Protect "spare" or emergency keys.

4. Equip outside doors with chain locks and peepholes.

5. Protect windows. Those adjoining fire escapes should prevent illegal entry but not prohibit emergency exit.

6. Know you neighbors and work together for mutual security.

7. Report anything peculiar such as faulty equipment or an unusual incident.

HOME SECURITY CHECKLIST

8. Do not admit anyone to the building with your remote door opener unless you know the person and purpose of the visit, and remind your child not to do so either!

9. Seek company on trips to a laundry room.

10. Do not ride self-service elevators with suspicious looking strangers, and do not let your child ride the elevators alone.

11. Use the emergency button if threatened in an elevator.

12. Alert the management, police and neighbors of the presence of unauthorized persons.

Recognizing Potential Dangers To And From School

WHEN GOING TO SCHOOL

School is not home! When your children are out of the house in the outside world they must remember at all times to use common sense street smarts. Teach them to be aware of their surroundings: to always keep one eye on the people and cars around them; to stay alert and aware. If your child is bullied, robbed, assaulted, abused, or touched in a way that he/she doesn't feel is right, make sure he/she knows to immediately report this to you, a teacher, or a trusted adult. Children need to know that adults can help, but only if they're asked to.

The daily routine of going to school and coming back takes about one-third of each day. Since your children are spending such a great deal of time out of your house, it's a good idea to be aware of some of the potential dangers out there. We don't place

very much importance on our routines. We don't think about them once they are established. This is a big mistake, because anyone who can familiarize him or herself with your routines can know your vulnerabilities.

Your child should never walk through anyone's backyard, even if you know whose home it is. Tell children never to walk down empty side streets or alleyways. There have been many cases of children being kidnapped or abused, last seen walking to or from school. If children do not pay attention to their surroundings, many things can go wrong. Children should follow these instructions: When walking, stay away from the side of the road, always use a sidewalk and walk facing the on-coming traffic. This way you can see the people and cars coming towards you. If you are riding your bike, don't take short-cuts, and stay in a group. Watch out for potholes, broken glass, or other potentially dangerous objects that could cause you to injure yourself. If you're hurt you become vulnerable.

The following walk-through will help you and your children rehearse what to do to be safe going to and from school.

WALK THROUGH ON A ONE DAY SECURITY EXPERIENCE

1. Have books and lunch together in one bag.
2. Is your bag closed? Is your personal ID in there, so you can identify it if it becomes mixed up with someone else's?
3. Do you have change (at least 2 quarters) for an emergency phone call?
4. Are your sneakers securely laced? Are the laces in good condition? It is very difficult to run with broken shoelaces or unlaced shoes.
5. Memorize your home telephone number and your father's and mother's office numbers.
6. Learn the location of the police station, fire station, and other locations such as a hospital, town hall or library. If running away from a stranger, you would have the advantage if you knew these locations.
7. Maintain a distance of at least 10 feet from adults you don't know.
8. If an adult calls you and asks that you go to them, do not get closer than 10 feet from them!
9. If an adult attempts to grab you, scream out: "THIS IS NOT MY FATHER/MOTHER!" as loud as you can and fight to get yourself released.
10. If an adult says, "Come with me, I am a policeman," remember to stand at least 10 feet away and tell them to come back in a police uniform and a police car. Always remember that the police, your parents, your school teachers and other authority figures want you to act this way.
11. Never leave school with a stranger.
12. Do not hitchhike to or from school.
13. Always report all crimes to the main office of school.
14. Keep all your lockers locked. Do not give your combination to anyone.
15. Never take a lot of cash or valuables to school.
16. Make sure your parents know when you leave school.

CARPOOLS

Whether you're the parent driving the carpool or some other parent picks up your children, the following precautions will keep everyone safe. Be sure all children in the carpool are introduced to all parents who may be driving, so that they feel secure going with that person.

Teach children to always have respect for the parents and other children in the carpool. They should be ready at the specified time so as not to keep the others waiting. This will ensure that everyone arrives on time and in good spirits. Children should carry the numbers of the parents who are driving them. That way, they can call to notify the parents if they will be late, preventing needless waiting and worrying. When your children leave the house, teach them to make sure that all windows and doors are securely locked and to turn off or unplug all appliances, TV, stereo, and other items they had been using. For the parents in the carpool, there are several ways to ensure every-

one's safety in and around your car. Once inside the car, lock all the doors and roll the windows up, and don't forget everyone's seatbelt. Be sure to fuel your car the night before so your gas tank is at least half full.

ALL CARS SHOULD BE EQUIPPED WITH THESE SAFETY ITEMS:
1. Spare tire and tire changing tools including a jack and tire-iron
2. Fire extinguisher
3. First aid kit
4. Flares
5. White flag
6. Blanket (in case you get stuck in the cold)
7. Additional repair tools (depending on your ability)

If for some reason you have car trouble, or you break down on the way to school, there are steps you should follow. First, pull off the road away from traffic. Raise the hood of your car, and tie a white flag on your antenna. Then get back into your car, lock the doors and await police help. Keep the vehicle in "park" with the emergency brake on and the engine off. If another motorist offers help, roll your window down slightly and ask them to call emergency road service, the police or a family member. Do not exit the car if possible. If you must change a tire, first put the emergency brake on, then block the tires so that the car will not roll off the jack and cause bodily harm or damage to your car. Be sure not to lock your keys in the trunk or in the car.

When dropping off the children, be aware of your surroundings. Look for any strangers hanging out in the schoolyard, or watching from across the street, or from another car. Before you drive off, be certain that everyone has made it safely into the school. Remember you are responsible for their lives; you are the adult that they were with last. When dropping the children off at home, again wait to make sure they enter their homes safely. If you are dropping off a latchkey kid, try to drop him off last so you can actually get out of your car and enter the house with the child. This way you know that he is in a safe house. Once again, you are the last person who has seen that child.

SCHOOL BUSES

If your children ride the bus to school, it's a good idea to arrive at the bus stop within 5 minutes of when the bus is due to arrive. A child alone out there, waiting for 20-30 minutes, is an easy target. Be as close to on time as possible. Be sure you and your child know the name of your driver, and that you can identify him/her. While on the bus, children should stay seated, and wear their seat belts. They should keep their bookbags next to them, or on the floor in front of them, and be sure not to forget them. If your child's books get into someone else's hands, this person/stranger has the ability to become a security threat. He or she will have your home address. If your child needs to take the late bus home from school, ask the driver to drop him/her off as close to home as possible. When your child gets off the bus, he/she should be aware of the surroundings. If anyone had been following the bus, or if there are any unusual people hanging-out, instruct your child to refuse to get off the bus.

If at all possible drop off and pick up your child from the bus stop. This is especially applicable to grammar-school children. You don't want to let your child walk alone. There have been too many cases of children being abducted when only walking a block or two from their house. If your child does walk to or from the bus stop, know the bus schedule. Ask the school to set up a policy of calling parents whose children don't come to school. Also be sure to have your child call you when he/she gets home.

BULLIES

Bullying can happen anywhere and at anytime: at school, on the playground, at home, or on the streets. Bullies can be boys, as well as girls, be young or old, short or tall.

Teach your children how to respond to and deflect a bully's advances. Explain to them that what a bully does is make them feel at a disadvantage, in order to scare them into doing, or giving up something he/she doesn't want to do, or give up. Bullies sometimes want belongings, money or just want to coerce your child into doing/taking something to/from someone else. They use threats of violence to get their point across.

Bullies like to focus their attacks on the differences in people. Color, shape, size, money, or where you live. They make themselves feel better or superior by putting others down.

Tell your children to act confident when confronted by a bully, even if they are afraid. They should judge the situation, and leave or avoid it if necessary. If your children tell others about the situation, the bully is likely to stop. Bullies work on the assumption that other kids will be afraid to tell on them. Above all, remind them that there's nothing wrong with them; it's the bullies who have the problem.

Potential Danger In Recreational Environments

Recreational environments include anything from the neighborhood park, the local mall, school yard, or bike trail, to an actual summer or winter break vacation. Parks provide a source of relaxation and recreation. Unfortunately they also provide a criminal or kidnapper with the relaxed attitude he/she needs to exploit the vulnerabilities of the unaware. An escape from our daily troubles can end up as a source of even greater difficulty, or even as a disaster.

Trouble can often be avoided by observing a few common-sense precautions. The key to survival is awareness. Even on vacations or trips, identify vulnerabilities and implement precautionary measures.

THE PLAYGROUND

Playgrounds are, without a doubt, a primary location where kidnapping occurs. Parents must always be on their guard for any suspicious activities or lurking strangers. Remember, it only takes a second for your child to disappear. Many children can easily be lured into situations where they can easily be abducted. Please refer back to the section on strangers and lures, and be certain your child is fully aware of the potential dangers that are around him/her. Don't allow your child to play with anyone you don't know. Don't take any chances. For example, a stranger may offer to swing your child on a swing. In a moment, he/she can grab your child and run off.

Design a firm set of boundaries for your child. Your child needs to stay clear of the park entrances and exits. Other potentially dangerous areas are near ponds, if the park has one, and roadways and bicycle paths. If you are having a picnic keep an eye on your children. They are much more important than the food. Unfortunately, abductors are very aware of parent's temporary lack or attention on their child.

Arming your child with a whistle or other noise making device could prove invaluable. This way your child can EASILY attract attention to him/herself in the event of an emergency.

Before allowing an older child to go to the park alone, walk through it with him/her. Be certain you and your child know the area well. Things to look for include: phones, lights, park officials or police officers, safe and well-built playground equipment, traffic, and a first-aid station.

Teach your child to stay alert and to be leery of strangers. Should he/she need assistance, instruct him/her to find a police officer or park official. Children shouldn't ask strangers for help. Too many children are abducted in similar situations. Your child should always let someone, their parents or their siblings, know their whereabouts, when they are leaving and when they will be back. Children should always wear a watch, and always have change for the phone.

Teach your child to yell—LOUDLY—if someone comes up to him/her and grabs him/her: "I don't know this person! Let me go! This isn't my mother/father!" When your children leave the park, they need to be aware of their surroundings, noting any cars or people present. And they should go directly home, using the most traveled and direct route.

SHOPPING MALLS

Shopping malls present a set of unique circumstances for which certain precautions must be taken. Your child is hardly at risk when in the act of shopping. However, this does not include the trip to and from the mall, hanging around with their friends, or waiting for a ride.

Teach children to be alert and aware of their environment, to always watch out for people lurking around the area. When waiting for a ride, children should secure themselves by waiting behind closed doors at the entrance/exit of the mall. This way, they cannot be thrown into a car or van as easily as if they were waiting on the sidewalk. Children should always stay with their friends. They are less likely to fall prey to an abductor when in a group than if they are alone.

BIKES

A bike takes your child places, to the mall, to school, and to see friends. Used properly, it can be your child's best friend. Used in the wrong way, it can cause a lot of trouble. Know the responsibilities of bicycle use and upkeep.

THE BEST WAY TO BE A GOOD BIKE RIDER IS TO PRACTICE. TEACH YOUR CHILDREN THE BASICS:

- *Ride on the right side of the street.*
- *Keep a safe distance from other vehicles.*
- *Bikes are driven safely with just one rider.*
- *When riding in a group, it's safest to ride single file.*
- *Using bike routes is much safer than using public roadways.*
- *Understand/obey traffic signals.*
- *Use proper hand signals*

Left turn: left arm straight out with your hand pointed left.

Right turn: left arm out, bend at the elbow and point your hand up.

Stop: left arm out, bend at the elbow and point your hand down, with your palm facing back.

In addition to the above basics, a child who rides at dusk or night needs to be highly visible. He/she should wear white, or light colored clothing. A reflective vest could be a life-saver. A white light on the front of the bike, and a red light on the back, should be part of any night riding accessories.

Being a dare-devil is not a smart move. It only increases the chances of accidents. Explain to your child that he/she may look cool, but should be more concerned with staying alive. Here are some stunts your child must avoid.

- *Riding with "no hands"*
- *Weaving in and out of traffic*
- *Hitchhiking (grabbing onto the tail of a car/truck)*
- *Jumping curbs*

ALWAYS KEEP YOUR CHILDREN'S BIKES IN TOP CONDITION. HERE ARE JUST A FEW CHECKS THAT YOU SHOULD MAKE OFTEN:

- *air pressure in tires*
- *bent or broken spokes*
- *brakes*
- *chain is clean and oiled*

Have your children's bikes overhauled once a year by a reputable bike shop. Remember if a bike has a problem, and you don't know how to fix it, take it to the shop. A bicycle can be very dangerous, even deadly, if fixed improperly.

Besides riding safely, and maintaining bikes properly, talk to your children about what to do with their bikes when they are parking somewhere. They should always chain and lock their bikes. The chain should be at least 3/8" thick with a very strong lock. The most secure way to park a bike is to lock the frame and the rear wheel together, and then loop the chain around a sturdy object like a tree or a bike rack. Try to lock it up in a well-travelled area that is brightly lit.

Other safety tips regarding children and bicycles are crucially important. Children should always wear a helmet. They should also always carry identification, change for an emergency phone call, and important phone numbers. Having a tire repair kit and bike pump with them is also smart.

FAMILY TRIPS

When you travel, you represent an easy target to criminals. You and your children are outside your normal environment, possibly in unfamiliar territory. You are isolated from friends and conventional support conveniences. Often entranced with the stimuli of the vacation, your guard is down. Your manner of dress, speech and actions identify you as a "tourist" or stranger to the environment because you are out of your element.

When traveling, you should assemble a careful, organized and complete priority checklist well in advance of your vacation. You can avoid losing, misplacing or forgetting an object or possession this way. If you are planning a family trip, gather the family together to create your priority checklist. By taking the time to arrange priorities, and by using the input of all family members, almost all details can be worked out with all sharing in the responsibilities.

Discuss the entire vacation from beginning to end, covering all possible scenarios. Discuss possible hazards, dangers and precautionary measures. Simply giving your children general directions like "stay close to me," or "avoid strangers" is not good enough. By discussing details of your trip, as well as possible hazardous scenarios, you are promoting responsibility, involvement, awareness and safety within your family. Allow your children to contribute. By encouraging children to become aware of what could happen in various scenarios, you start them on the road to individual awareness of possible danger.

PRECAUTIONARY MEASURES-HOME SECURITY WHILE ON VACATION

Too many homes are the targets of vandals and thieves while the home owners are on vacation. An empty home is an enticing target for a thief. A home that appears occupied, or at least attended by someone, presents a discouraging target for a thief, vandal or burglar. Before departing for your trip, inform local police, your landlord, friends and family members of your trip and request that they keep a watchful eye on your home in your absence. Leave your home key with someone you trust, asking friends and family to report any suspicious activity to the police. Stop all newspapers and mail deliveries, or arrange to have the deliveries picked up by someone in your absence. If gone for more than a week, consider having the lawn cut, or in winter, having the snow removed from your driveway and walkways. Make sure a friend, neighbor or family member leaves trash in your trashcan for regular pick up, giving the home the appearance of occupation. If you can leave a vehicle parked in your regular driveway spot, do so. Leave all window blinds and shades in their normal position. If you don't have a timer on your home lighting, make sure someone can turn on both the inside and outside lights of your home. Don't discuss your plans for a vacation or trip in casual conversation or in a public locale, except with highly trusted friends or relatives. Never leave notes on any doors saying you are away or out for the day.

FAMILY IDENTIFICATION

If you are planning a family trip or vacation, be sure to supply each family member with some form of personal identification. Parents usually make sure their children never leave their side, but what would you do if your child somehow got separated from you? An identification card can be made for your children encased in plastic, and pinned to an article of clothing. This identification card should include pertinent information such as blood type, allergies, medication or health problems, in addition to the address and phone number of your current accommodations. In addition to this card, a daily family itinerary card should be carried on each child's person. This should contain temporary information such as vehicle I.D., where the family is, and the planned itinerary for the day.

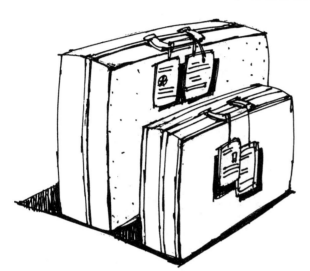

Give your children their personal I.D. card and itinerary, and then instruct them about what they must do if they get separated from you. Tell them to look for a police officer, security guard or similar official if possible. If at a park, tell them not to leave the park alone under any circumstances. Make sure everyone understands the activities planned and the time schedule for the activities. This way, each knows the others' location if separated. Each family member should make an effort to remember what type of clothes the others are wearing. Never split up the group leaving one child alone. Each parent must assume responsibility for one half of the group. Inform others when you're going to use a restroom. It's not a bad idea to locate and identify a policeman or security person, and point him/her out to your children, in case of emergency.

If you are planning an extended trip by car, consider additional safety tips. First, have your car checked out by a reputable mechanic to assure that it can safely make the trip. This includes checking tires, brakes, all hoses, fan belt, the battery and all fluids. It might be a good idea to join "Triple A" (AAA) or another reputable auto club for the convenience of 24-hour emergency road service. Avoid driving long distances without periodic breaks. Try to drive during the daylight hours if you are traveling long distances, and try to keep your gas tank as full as possible. This will enable you to reach large towns with open gas stations. If you are traveling on busy highways, convenient rest stops, gas stations and even restaurants are available for your use.

If you must drive at night, avoid short cuts and deserted back roads. Avoid hanging clothes in the back seat. Use your trunk if possible because clothes hanging in the back seat indicate you are traveling. Keep cameras and other valuables out of sight. Finally, make sure you have proper road maps, a spare tire, several flashlights, a dependable jack and flares to help ensure your safety.

If the family is planning to travel by plane, bus or any other public carrier there are several measures to consider. If traveling by bus or train, get a map of your route so everyone in the family understands your travel route, stops and transfers.

Realize that bus and subway terminals are frequented by criminals in search of likely victims. Try to plan your trip avoiding long waits in these dangerous areas. Stay in crowded, well-lit areas, in view of uniformed employees, and beware of strangers asking directions.

When seated, keep your bags in your lap, not on the floor or the next seat. Be aware of the people around you. If someone acts suspicious or threatening to you or your child, inform an official. If traveling by subway, be sure to stay a safe distance from the edge of the platform. The subway platform is a favorite location for purse snatchers and muggers. Stay alert at all times. Remember that the criminal always chooses the victim according to vulnerability. Keep your child at your side at all times. Have him/her hold your hand, or hold onto his/her arm. It is very easy to get separated in a crowded location. Don't present the image of an easy target, and you will most likely be left alone.

Make sure your baggage is locked and marked with complete identification on both the inside and outside. Remove all old tags. Never leave carry-on luggage unattended. Insure your valuables and credit cards, and avoid carrying large sums of cash. The most likely time to lose your baggage is before it's checked in, and after it is unloaded from the bus, train or plane. Try to keep your baggage in sight as much as possible. When you arrive at your destination go directly to the baggage claim area, and pick up your luggage and other baggage. This could help prevent your belongings from being stolen.

VACATION SECURITY

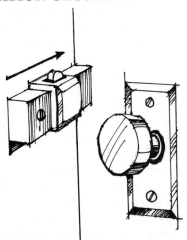

When staying out-of-state remember you are in unfamiliar territory. Your vehicle license plate identifies you as a stranger, making you a prime target for the local criminal. This criminal also realizes you probably won't stay long, not long enough to report a missing camera or similar item to the local authorities. Unfortunately, the room key you are issued when checking in isn't the only key that opens your door. Other copies exist. In addition, most hotel room locks can be opened with a credit card or spatula. Discourage your child from divulging information to others, such as where you'll be staying and for how long.

Unless your hotel doors have additional locks, such as a dead-bolt, door chain and door viewer, you might consider improvising certain protective measures of your own.

For example, a chair wedged with the back of the chair against the door knob is an effective safety precaution while you are in your room. A simple rubber door-wedge can be inserted under the door, effectively preventing the door from being opened from either side. Purchased at any hardware store, these provide practical, economical, portable safety. There are a variety of portable travel locks available on the market today. When used, the door cannot be opened unless broken down. It's up to you to decide what you require for peace of mind while away from home.

The following checklist will help you quickly review the security tips you need to consider to ensure your vacation is a safe and joyous one.

WHEN GOING ON VACATION

1. Make your house look lived in.
2. Remind your children not to tell their friends the specifics of your vacation, i.e. date of departure, location, or date of return.
3. Notify the police and your neighbors.
4. Stop mail, newspapers, and any other deliveries to your home.
5. Be sure to set a timer switch for inside and outside door lights.
6. Make the outside of your house look lived in: cut grass, shovel snow, and, if possible, keep cars in driveways.
7. Arrange to have your dog fed, and walked at home rather than kept at a kennel. If you don't have a dog, having someone you trust water your plants serves the same purpose of having your home look "lived in."
8. Arrange for garbage and trash to be put out and picked up as usual.
9. Arrange for secure storage of furs, jewelry and other valuables outside your house while you are away.
10. Have your home's alarm system checked before leaving.
11. Avoid publicity about your pending trip.
12. Do not pack your car the night before departure; load it quickly in the morning.
13. Before leaving, check to see that all doors and windows are locked.

Violence Against Children

Many situations outside the home are potentially dangerous. But most of us are lucky enough to feel safe in our homes. For a child reared in a happy home, the home represents a safe haven, a place of warmth, love and security. For an abused child, the home becomes a prison; the child's life becomes a nightmare.

One unfortunate repercussion of abuse in the home is often criminal behavior. This isn't to say that all of today's battered children are tomorrow's criminals. Yet there is something to be said for the correlation between domestic violence and crime. Not only is the initial act of child abuse a crime, with repetition over years, the hostility and anti-social tendencies displayed to the child become ingrained, part of the child's nature. It is both unrealistic and irresponsible to think that constant, severe beatings, or even continual berating won't take an emotional toll on any child, manifesting itself in some way later in life.

CHILD ABUSE

Statistics show that over 3.2 million children are abused annually. Over fifty percent of the criminals who commit crimes against children were victims of some kind of abuse earlier in their lives. Thus, the acts of child abuse in the home eventually affect all of us in one way or another. If one family's domestic violence brings repercussions to another family years later (potentially with the loss of a life), obviously the issue of child abuse and the need for prevention concern everyone. Domestic violence is a more common problem than previously believed. And even though domestic violence is not a new problem, recent increases in media exposure have brought greater awareness of the extent of domestic violence.

In years past, neighbors and other well-intentioned persons refrained from reporting child abuse. One reason was fear of legal retaliation. Please realize that no one can be prosecuted for acting in good faith when someone's safety is concerned. There are laws requiring law enforcement officials, teachers, social workers and day care providers to report all or any signs of domestic violence. The specifics of what legally constitutes abuse are determined by individual states. If you ever suspect the abuse of a child, choose to err on the side of caution. Call the local child advocacy office. Child abuse can be defined as the continued abuse or neglect of a child by the child's legal guardian.

Another reason why people fail to report domestic violence is due to ignorance and lack of exposure to and awareness of the problem. But these days seeing the causes and effects of domestic violence on the daily news, it is easier for all of us to identify similar or possible signs pointing to abuse of some kind.

Child abuse occurs for many different reasons. Perhaps a parent is under great stress due to financial burdens. Feeling badly about the inability to meet financial obligations can cause frustration, anger and abuse. An unhappy marriage is often the cause. Perhaps one or both partners experience a great deal of stress due to a lack of harmony between them, causing verbal or physical conflict. Not only is this a poor example for the children, hostility between parents can easily turn and focus on children.

Another cause of child abuse is drug or alcohol abuse. The inability to deal with life's problems is self-evident in the drug or alcohol abuser, and his or her lack of self-control and common sense is obvious. If you know any parent who is a drug or alcohol abuser, and you notice signs of child abuse or neglect, don't be afraid to report it.

Child abuse is not confined to the home environment. The school, work and play environments of a child could also be the source of possible child abuse.

EMOTIONAL ABUSE

Emotional abuse ranges from obvious and extreme insults and degradations to more subtle forms. Emotional abuse often results from a parent's lack of interest in the child's life, performance at school or relationships. This type of parent spends little time with his/her children, and has little or no interest in being a proper role model. Much of what children absorb in the home in the areas of emotional health and behavior is learned by example. The children who receive no emotional support from their parents may not suffer immediately, but will manifest problems later in life: inability to communicate, anti-social behavior, or lack of morals, no sense of right and wrong.

Victims of abuse need help, whether they realize they need it or not. Reporting any suspected abuse or neglect is not a violation of anyone's privacy or civil rights. It is your duty as a concerned citizen and fellow human.

VERBAL ABUSE

This type of abuse is not confined to any social class or income. It is due to a lack of love, guidance or because of emotional instability on the part of the abusive parent. Constant criticism, verbally displayed favoritism towards one child over another, the display of extreme anger in front of a child, blaming a child for a problem or mistake, or actual verbal threats are examples of verbal abuse.

PHYSICAL ABUSE

The term "physical abuse" brings continued or unwarranted beatings to mind first. Courts do not convict parents for slapping a child's hand or disciplining a child for bad behavior. Therefore discipline becomes abuse when it is continual and unwarranted. Bruises, welts, discoloration of the eye area, bloody noses or lips are often signs of possible child abuse.

You may not want to interfere in your neighbor's privacy at the first sign of injury. Some energetic children have been known to be accident-prone. But look at the injury closely if you can. Skinned knees or hands, bruises on the lower leg or scratches may not be indications of abuse. Black and blue marks, swollen eyes or mouths, injured wrists or marks on the upper body may be an indication of child abuse. Remain keenly aware and report potential abuse if your instincts tell you those kids could be in jeopardy.

Another form of physical child abuse is neglect: depriving a child of proper food, water and good nutrition. Even more extreme is the lack of shelter or clothing. Depriving a child of a late snack as a form of discipline, or simply failing to cater to a spoiled child is a far cry from a pattern of continually sending a child to bed without dinner as a punishment, or failing to provide enough food. Some forms of child abuse are intentional and others are unintentional. The result is the same: physical and emotional injury or death.

If the parents fail to or refuse to recognize a problem, even if the parents themselves aren't the cause, what recourse does an abused child have? It is important that all children be taught about the possibility of abuse, the punishment for it, and the importance of reporting any abuse (their own or a friend's) immediately. In the case of domestic abuse, often a relative, neighbor or friend files the report.

Enrolling your child in a self-defense school or martial arts dojo (school) is a way for your child to learn defensive tactics. The awareness of possible abuse combined with the ability to defend him/herself gives your child a margin of safety that can make a difference.

Naturally a child cannot hope to beat an adult attacker into submission. However, all adults have vulnerable areas of the body, and children can deliver blows there if necessary. Strikes to the eyes, throat, nose or groin can definitely put an attacker at a severe disadvantage. Once the attacker is stunned, the child can hopefully escape and report the crime to the proper authority or his/her parents.

SEXUAL ABUSE

Sexual abuse was kept quiet for many years. This has changed recently, and today you cannot read the paper or watch television news without hearing of it. As with other forms of abuse, it can be the behavior of a similarly abused parent, but this is not always the case. Often those we trust with the care of our children are responsible. Even older children have been known to abuse younger children. If you ever see or suspect such a situation, take immediate steps to remedy the problem. If a child shows signs of being in pain when sitting, walking or performing bodily functions, these could be possible signs of sexual abuse. Other signs are rage or anger, anti-social behavior, preferring isolation to company, a problem forming or maintaining friendships, fighting, quarreling, manipulative behavior and low self-esteem. Often a child's reluctance to go to school, his/her dislike of a teacher, or failure to participate in any activity is due to fear. This fear should be addressed and dealt with, not ignored or glossed over. Often a child abuse victim feels guilty, or afraid to reveal what happened. Sometimes this is because he/she fears the parent's reaction; other times it is the actual abuser he/she fears. In either case, if a child shows fear or reluctance to go anywhere without you, or be in the care of other adults or older children, stop and question him/her. The child may not reveal what occurred at first. He or she may have been violated in a terrible way, and is perhaps not even old enough to understand what happened. Slow, patient questioning may get the child to reveal the abuse.

RAPE

Rape is usually thought to refer to a man forcing a woman to have sex against her will. That definition only covers some rapes. Men, children, the young and the old can be victims of rape.

Rape, by definition, is "the carnal knowledge of a female forcibly and against her will." Possibly one of the most misunderstood crimes, rape leaves the victim suffering from physical and long-term psychological trauma. Among the physical effects of rape are: internal and external injury, pregnancy, venereal disease, AIDS, and even death. The emotional toll taken on the rape victim is equally serious as rage, humiliation, fear, alienation and ostracism from the community make it difficult for victims to heal mentally and emotionally.

According to the FBI, a rape is attempted or committed once every five minutes in the United States. Rape is both a violent crime and a sexual assault. Sexual desire is rarely the motivation for rape. It is an act of rage, a desire on the part of the rapist to control, humiliate and injure. Many states consider all acts of forced sexual contact equal to rape (including rape committed against men by other men or women). Regardless of who the rape victim is, the effects are similar. No one should ever be forced to submit to sexual contact against his/her will. This is violent humiliation taken to the extreme. And the humiliation exists for the victim long after the rape is over, when dealing with the emotional repercussions of the crime.

For some rape victims, denial is a way to deal with the emotional impact of what has occurred. The ordeal of re-living the experience when having to report the rape is often too traumatic for the victim. He or she may feel that simply not thinking about what happened will make the problem disappear. Perhaps the victim keeps silent because he/she knows the rapist, and for some reason cannot divulge the rapist's identity. Under no circumstances should you keep silent if you have been sexually assaulted in any way! Please realize that the rapist will do it again (to you or somebody else) if he sees he/she can get away with it.

Similar to the long term effects of child abuse, rape fosters hostility and mistrust in the victim, which affects the way the victim relates to the outside world. If you have been assaulted or raped (or if you know someone who has) report it to the authorities. Keeping silent about any form of sexual abuse is a mistake. Not reporting enables the rapist to rape again. The victim is denying him/herself the satisfaction of justice that is his/her right by law.

In the event of the rape of a child, years and years of mistrust and anger and fear, healing and therapy may ensue. Can you think of a more hateful crime than the rape of a child? Love and more love may be the only cure. Bandaged by patience, tolerance and understanding the child may someday heal.

RECOGNIZING CHILD ABUSE

1. Learn to recognize the signs of child abuse: frequent cuts, bruises, welts or broken bones.

2. Learn to recognize odd behavior in the child: anger, anti-social tendencies, or reluctance to be in another adult's care.

3. Report child abuse to the police and your local welfare agency.

If you are a victim and wish to make a report, have your parents or neighbors take pictures of your injuries while they're still fresh. Make copies of hospital reports or bills, and remember the names of the people you reported the abuse to. You may need them as witnesses someday.

NOTE TO CHILDREN

If you are personally being abused, tell your parents or teacher or call the police. It will be hard for you to report someone you know, especially your parents, but it will be harder for you to continue being abused. Your parents need help and guidance. You don't have to live with the pain. Abuse is not your fault!

Don't be a victim! If you are an abused child, there are places you can go. Contact the police or ask for help from a trusted neighbor or friend. If you have little brothers or sisters, think of them and report the abuse—the sooner you tell, the sooner it will stop, the sooner you will heal.

REPORTING CHILD ABUSE

Abusive parents often fail to recognize their own abusive behavior. If they do recognize the problem, they may choose to ignore it, to deny it. Children rarely volunteer to report abuse. They feel alienated, without a friend. Sometimes the abused child is left feeling guilty, as if the abuse was deserved. Similarly wives often cannot bring themselves to report abuse against them. They have been so degraded, so beaten down emotionally and physically that they have no strength or self-confidence to pick up the phone and ask for help.

Any type of abuse you strongly suspect should be reported. If you are considering reporting an abuser consider the following:

1. Have you noticed a repeating pattern of abuse, or just one incident?

2. Are your observations unbiased? If so, contact your local welfare department to report the case. If you suspect a child is in immediate danger do not hesitate to call the police.

When reporting, remember to give your name if possible. If for some reason you prefer to remain anonymous that is your option, although the police won't have any witness to the crime should they need to question you later, which may be important for a trial or hearing. But a child's life is more important, so do not hesitate to call the police if you fear for any child's safety.

Streetwise Self-defense for Children

INTRODUCTION

Learning a martial art such as Karate, Ju-Jitsu, Tae Kwon Do or other form of self-defense is a smart way to learn how to defend yourself. It is also a good way to stay in shape and learn discipline, confidence, control, awareness, and—if you want—how to be competitive.

The first time my father brought me into a dojo (self-defense school), I felt lucky and proud. My father had a high ranking in the martial arts and he was going to train me. That didn't make it any easier, if anything, it made it tougher. I was seven years old then, and even though my two older brothers were already learning from my father, I have to admit I was still scared. My father always wanted us to be the best and made us work twice as hard to achieve that goal.

I remember putting on my first *gi* (uniform) and my father taking me to the mat and explaining that respect for the arts is one of the most important steps to learning them. He showed me how to bow before stepping onto the mat (karate deck) and said that you must wait for the ranking Dan (black belt) to bow back to you. Only then do you have permission to enter the class.

What frightened me the most about the martial arts were the throwing techniques used in Jujitsu and Judo. Actually, it was being thrown that worried me. It looked as if the students were really hurting each other! But my father explained to me that it's the way you fall that will determine if you get hurt or not. That is why learning how to fall and mastering the different falling techniques (Ukemi) is so important.

The martial arts are like anything else worthwhile. They take time and a lot of practice to master. Before I made my first forward roll, my father warned me to go slowly. Of course, like the big know-it-all, the Sensei's (teacher) son, I ran down the mat and rolled flat on my head. It sure hurt, but I think my pride was hurt more.

My father came over to me and said, "You're not going to get anywhere unless you take it slowly." He made me go back and do it again and again, until I got it right. I learned that when you take your time and master the proper way to do things, they become much easier and almost automatic.

At first, all the martial arts may seem the same to you, and they are similar to an extent, but they are also very different. Karate emphasizes kicks and punches (open-handed and closed-fisted strikes). It is said that a Karate master can defend himself against an attacker twice his size. Jujitsu, the mother of all the oriental martial arts, is a form of self-defense incorporating the techniques of wrist locks, holds, and throws. Judo is basically stand-up wrestling, with its use of grappling techniques and throws. It is a very clean sport, a true one-to-one sport. That is probably why Judo is included in the Olympics. Maybe one day, an American athlete will win the gold metal. It could be you.

By studying the techniques of these ancient disciplines, you will not only develop physically, but mentally as well. Once you decide to undertake the study of self-defense, you must learn to endure a tough routine of exercises and master very specific controlled physical movements. Through rigorous practice of these movements, you will train your mind and body to react as one, to develop into a well-tuned machine. In turn, you will develop a sense of special confidence, and a positive attitude.

If you really want to learn how to protect yourself against attackers and be confident, I recommend a self-defense class. I know it made a difference in my life and I'm glad I started early. If I can do it after falling on my head, you can surely do it.

BASIC TECHNIQUES

Before you can defend yourself adequately, you must learn and practice certain basic techniques—the building blocks of self-defense. As you master these basic techniques and acquire new knowledge and skills, your awareness of mental and physical powers will also grow, and you will develop the total coordination and muscle control you need to defend yourself with confidence.

If you are serious about learning to defend yourself, you will put as much effort and concentration into it as you can. I strongly recommend that you devote at least one hour a day to the practice of the basic stances, blocks, strikes, and falls. If you get involved in self-defense heavily enough, you will find within your mind and body the inner strength that can come only from dedicated practice. This inner force has been called "Ki" by the Japanese. The essence of this difficult concept lies in the idea that the strength of a person cannot be determined by physical strength alone. Both mind and body must be unified before true power can be achieved. From time to time we hear of people who perform amazing feats of strength in moments of great stress; for example, someone lifts a car to free someone who is trapped. The only reason the person is able to lift the car is that his or her mind and body, which normally function separately, are instinctively unified.

Before we move on to the basic blocks, strikes, and falls, let us look for a moment at the importance of "Kiai" to your self-defense. In practical terms, "Kiai" is a loud shout that you should incorporate into all your practice sessions. If you are grabbed by an attacker, a loud, self-asserting yell will very probably frighten or shock your assailant, giving you an advantage and throwing your attacker momentarily off balance. "Kiai" is more, however, than a mere shock tactic. "Kiai" is both psychologically and physiologically effective. The expulsion of air through your lungs increases your strength. It is not enough just to yell; you must expel all the air from your throat and diaphragm. You should be able to feel all your muscles tighten at the moment of expulsion. Properly done, a "Kiai" will help you attain maximum strength while at the same time frightening your attacker.

If your child finds him/herself in a situation where he/she is being kidnapped, instead of using a "Kiai," he/she should yell: "He's not my mother/father!"

Parents and children must practice this at home. Surprise your child by grabbing him, and have him practice his "Kiai." Fifteen minutes every day should be devoted to practicing self-defense moves. This may not only save your child's life, but will lead to proficiency, increased self-awareness and confidence in your child.

Practice "Kiai" with all the basic movements: strikes, blocks, and falls. Tell your children not to be embarrassed; it may someday save their lives.

You can begin your child's practice for self-defense at home, using a mirror, until your child feels comfortable in his/her movements. Use the horse rider's stance as the starting point for blocks and hand strikes. (For kicks you will use the other three basic stances: the forward stance, cat stance, and side stance). As you progress and gain confidence, find someone to be your child's partner. Siblings make great practice partners. They can take turns assuming the attacker's role and practicing the basic defenses described in this book.

Let us take a look at the positions of the hand that your child will use for most of the strikes and grabs in his/her self-defense arsenal. The hands are two of the most important weapons humans have. There are many different hand positions and strikes beyond the traditional fist punch. With the hand held flat, one can use the fingertips to thrust or chop with either edge of the hand (the "knife-edge" or the "inside knife-edge"). The illustrations show the portions of the hand used to deliver the blow. With the hand in a fist position, your child can strike with the knuckles straight on or with the backfist; he/she can strike down or across with the hammerfist and reverse hammerfist. He/she can open a fist part way and strike with the heel of his/her hand. A variation of this strike is the "palm hand" strike, in which a hand is cupped. Finally, by opening the cup into a claw, your child is ready for a "claw hand strike," usually aimed at the eyes or the Adam's apple. As you practice these strikes in the mirror with your child, go slowly and concentrate on form and balance; speed and self-confidence will follow.

Kicks may be delivered with the ball or heel of your foot, with either side of your foot, or with the instep. You may kick up or sideways, or you may punch with your foot. You can use the side of a shoe or its heel to rake or scrape an attacker if he has you from behind, and of course you can stamp down on his instep.

In addition to the offensive movements, you should incorporate defensive movements into each practice session. In the following pages you will see a dozen blocks and falls illustrated. You can practice these movements alone, but you should use a partner as soon as possible. Again, begin slowly and concentrate on balance and form. When you practice blocks, get used to using them when moving forward and when falling back. If you are attacked, you must always move forward if you see the strike coming in time, and move backward when the strike is already moving quickly toward you. You should move immediately from a block into a strike or a fall.

As you acquire self-confidence and ability, you should build the goal of developing a continuous series of movements into your practice sessions. If you are attacked, you will not make a move and wait to see what happens; you must carry out a constant counterattack until you are out of danger. The strikes you will be practicing are done while the attacker has you in a bear hug one from behind, one from the front. Practice each series first to the left side and then to the right. Do all the strikes in succession, slowly at first, then with moderate speed, and finally with full speed. You should begin, as you gain confidence, to develop a definite sense of where and how to strike and how much force to use. Again, practicing with your children—perhaps even taking simultaneous self-defense classes—will help not just them, but you too.

STRIKES AGAINST VULNERABLE AREAS

In this chapter, we will deal with the natural weapons of your body (your hands, feet, elbows, and knees) and with the vulnerable target areas of your attacker's body. Neither the size of these natural weapons nor your own physical strength is the major factor in immobilizing an attacker. It is, rather, the precise timing and delivery of a strike to a vital area that makes it effective. What about the amount of force needed to stop an attacker? If you are attacked, you must strike as hard and as fast as you can, for the attacker is out to hurt you. But remember that it is your form and speed which are the major sources of the force you have available. With practice, you will soon realize that you have sufficient force to defend yourself and to immobilize an attacker if you have to. The techniques you are acquiring are designed specifically to maximize the force delivered by a strike. The target areas you will become familiar with are all highly vulnerable. In the illustrations that follow, you will see which blows are likely to be most effective against the various vulnerable target areas on your attacker, from his eyes to his feet. First, however, let us review what damage you can do with a well-aimed hand, foot, elbow, or knee.

You can counterattack easily to many areas above your attacker's shoulders. His eyes, ears, nose, temples, forehead, and neck all are very vulnerable. Any blow to these areas will cause great pain and may well disable an attacker. A strike to the eyes with a book, lunch box, bat, or stick, can easily cause temporary or permanent blindness. A blow to the nose can knock a man out; or at least it will cause his eyes to water uncontrollably. A cupped hand strike to the ears can rupture the eardrum. With proper power and aim to the front or side of the throat you can cause severe damage to the organs located there. If you strike your attacker at the back of the neck, especially with your elbow, as you are being picked up from the waist, you can cause whiplash or a broken neck. Do not worry about what you may do to the attacker; remember what he is trying to do to you, and remember that he will do it if you don't stop him first!

The trunk of the body provides larger and more readily available targets. Just a moderate blow to the rib cage can break some ribs. If ribs are broken, at the very least your attacker will have trouble breathing, and you will gain time to continue your counterattack or to escape. Below the rib cage, you can attack the diaphragm, solar plexus, kidneys, spleen, bladder, and groin. Striking in the diaphragm (the mid-section, just below the frontal rib cage) can knock the wind out of an attacker, leaving him at your mercy. Any such injury could send your attacker into shock. Blows to the kidneys, to the spleen on the left side of the abdomen, to the bladder, and to the groin might cause internal bleeding, leading to nausea, pain, and/or dizziness.

Your attacker's limbs are vulnerable also. A broken elbow or knee cap is extremely painful and immobilizing. A hard blow on the shin or foot can splinter the bone and temporarily stop your attacker. Remember that after any blow to a limb, even an effective one, you will have to follow up with another strike and possibly another.

Study and learn the strikes and targets in this chapter and put them together into patterns of continuous movement. Each blow is not just a blow in self-defense. It is a step toward the next blow. You must teach your children to be prepared to fight until they are out of danger.

USING YOUR PERSONAL ITEMS AS WEAPONS

Whether you know it or not, many objects your children carry to school or at the playground or to recreational events can be used as weapons against an attacker. Things like lunch boxes, book bags, a comb, football helmet, bat or hockey stick can all be used as weapons. They become important defensive tools not only for your children, but for adults as well. Abductors, rapists, bullies, child molesters, and robbers come in all shapes and sizes. Many are men, many are women. Preparing your children in the event that they are attacked/approached, is the key.

Always have these items ready to use. For example when carrying a football helmet, your child should hold it by the face-guard. This way it is ready to be swung, if need be. A baseball bat, or hockey stick should be held by the narrow end of the bat or stick. When walking to and from the field, carry it over your shoulder, or in a position that you feel is most comfortable for you to be able, at a moment's notice, to use it against someone. Do not carry your shoes/glove on the end of your bat/stick. This will hinder movement/momentum if you need to swing it. If you have a coke bottle, lunch box, set of keys, or book-bag, always have them in a position to use if necessary. Your bike chain/lock, skateboard, roller blades, or ice-skates should also be carried so you can swing them at someone if necessary. Whistles or noise makers become an important item especially when you have someone suspicious coming at you.

Preparing your child for situations that can occur in your community is an important parenting responsibility. You cannot be with your children 24 hours a day, so it's your responsibility to teach them how to protect themselves.

We all want to believe that an attack will never happen to us. But reality has proven that myth wrong, and it's time to understand what we need to do to fight back.

HOW TO PREVENT INJURIES

In the martial arts (as in any sport), you are naturally in a situation where you might get injured. Most injuries can be prevented by using protective equipment, keeping alert to your opponent, and by studying the proper techniques. While practicing the martial arts, never catch your partner by surprise or fool around when you should be serious.

As you begin your training there is a possibility of muscle soreness or injury. Stretching exercises are necessary to limber up the body. Whenever you do a new exercise or movement, you use muscles that are not accustomed to the activity. As a result, they will become sore. Do not let this discourage you from working out. As you repeat the same exercises and movements, your muscles begin to strengthen and develop.

The best indication of limbered-up muscles is a feeling of warmth throughout your body. This means you are ready to go.

Occasionally, it is difficult to detect an injury since it may not hurt right away. However, if you do feel any pain, have a hard time moving one of your muscles or joints, or if you see some swelling or a bruise, be sure to rest and notify your doctor. Never work out when you feel pain; you will only make your injury worse.

THESE BASIC RULES SHOULD BE FOLLOWED WHEN YOU WORK OUT:

1. *Take your time. Don't rush your exercises. Warming up is essential for all athletes.*
2. *Always concentrate on what you are doing. Don't let your mind wander.*
3. *If you are tired, don't force yourself to work out. Most injuries occur when you don't have the energy to exercise properly, and your body needs rest.*

4. *Never over-train. Only work out to your limit. Forcing yourself will just make you weak.*

5. *Never eat a large meal immediately before or after you work out. Always wait at least a half-hour, so that your body will be able to digest the food properly.*

A WORD ABOUT NUTRITION

Although exercise and self-defense training are important methods for maintaining physical fitness, they cannot be performed without adhering to a proper diet.

When the word diet is used, it does not only refer to a low-caloric intake. As you exercise and burn up calories, as well as needed nutrients, you have to replace them by eating three well-balanced meals per day. This is especially important for children whose bodies are still growing.

Food is fuel for the body. Without it, your body cannot perform and develop properly. If your body lacks proteins or other nutrients and minerals, you will not achieve the muscle development or tone that is the goal of exercise. You will fatigue easily and become susceptible to excessive soreness. Avoid junk foods (empty calories) and eat foods that are rich in the nutrients and minerals your body needs (non-fatty meats, chicken, fish, vegetables, milk, cheese, eggs, whole-wheat breads, and cereals, nuts, fruits, and raisins for snacks). Remember, do not go overboard on any one food. Follow a varied diet.

In your martial arts self-defense training, you will demand a lot from your body. Feed it well!

Combat Drills For Practicing Your Self Defense

In these upcoming pictures you will be shown combat drills for developing your speed, focus and control while learning physical self-defense. Keep in mind that you must be careful when practicing these drills.

Combat drills #1

A1. *Face one another in the fighting stance.*

A2. *The first move is to push your attacker's hand down.*

A3. *Pull the lead hand out and push your attacker's hand down.*

A4. *Complete the move by punching to the opposite side of your attacker's face with your left hand.*

Combat drills #2

B1. *Assume a fighting stance.*

B2. *Push the left elbow to your opponent's right side.*

B3. *Pull the left hand back and punch the rib cage with your right hand.*

B4. *Complete the move by punching the left side of your opponent's face.*

Combat Drill #3

C1. *Assume a fighting stance.*

C2. *Grab your opponent's left arm.*

C3. *Now perform a lead roundhouse kick.*

C4. *Now punch directly across your opponent's face.*
NOTE: Be very cautious with your contact, never use full force on your partner.

Combat Drill #4

D1. *Assume a combat fighting stance.*

D2. *Grab your opponent's wrist.*

D3. *Perform a lead roundhouse kick.*

D4. *Punch to the left side of your opponent's face.*

D5. *Complete the move with a careful wrist-locking technique.*

Street and Playground Self-defense

It is important for all children to learn how to use different sports and playground items for self-defense. These illustrations show you how a single hockey stick or stickball bat can save you from a dangerous situation. We will also show you playground self-defense using simple open hand techniques.

DEFENSE WITH A SKATEBOARD

1. The attacker confronts you in the playground while you have your skateboard in your hand.

2. As he goes to grab you, you immediately bring the skateboard up, striking to the side of his head.

3. You finish the move by kicking the attacker in the shin for a quick getaway.

DEFENSE WITH A STICKBALL BAT

1. Your attacker is grabbing to pull you forward.

2. As he pulls you forward you flip the stickball bat up to your left open hand and drive it directly into his stomach.

3. You now turn the bat over and strike your attacker to the head to complete the move.

DEFENSE WITH A HOCKEY STICK

1. Your attacker is grabbing you by the shoulder, bullying you.

2. Bringing the hockey stick over his arm as you grab the other end of the stick with your left hand, you drive the stick down toward your body.

3. As your attacker starts to pull away you complete the move by driving the hockey stick up into his face.

OPEN HAND TECHNIQUES

1A. *Your attacker attempts to grab you and pull you to him.*

2A. *As he pulls you forward drive your fingers into his eyes (don't forget to scream out loud to attract attention).*

NOTE: After completing your defensive attacks get away from your attacker and yell for help as you run.

3A. *You complete the move by driving your foot directly up between your attacker's legs into his groin.*

1B. *Your attacker attempts to grab you by the shoulder and pull you toward him in a possible kidnapping situation.*

2B. *Lift your left foot as you hang onto his hands so he cannot get away. Then, drive a side kick into his knee cap. After completing the strike, yell for help as you run.*

1C. *As your attacker attempts to grab you by the hair or back of the head you immediately use you outside forearm block.*

2C. *As you have applied the block you quickly rotate the arm around locking up on his right arm as you attack with an open clawhand strike to the throat.*

3C. *You complete the move by driving your knee up into your attacker's groin. This should immobilize him long enough to get help.*

1D. *Your attacker is grabbing you by the shirt, threatening to hurt you.*

2D. *You're grabbing his wrist preparing to quickly strike your attacker. Holding onto his right wrist you strike to the stomach.*

3D. *You complete the move by driving your knee directly to your attacker's stomach as you grab the back of his head.*

1E. *Your attacker has his hands around your throat.*

2E. *From this angle, as he pulls you forward, drive your elbow into his mid-section as hard as you can. This will surprise your attacker.*

3E. *To complete this move you quickly turn your body, strike to his throat and his groin*

1F. *As your attacker grabs you in a front bear hug you strike your head to his ankle or instep.*

2F. *You then drive upward to his groin with your knee.*

3F. *You then strike with a palm hand to his ears.*

4F. *As you turn around completely grab him around the neck.*

5F. *Complete the move with a grappling position.*

FRONTAL ATTACK

1G. *Your attacker is attempting to grab you or hit you. You quickly block.*

2G. *Immediately drive both hands under his chin while hooking his leg to throw him backward.*

3G. *Complete the move by striking with your foot if necessary.*

FRONT CHOKE OR GRAB

1H. *Your attacker attempts to grab you.*

2H. *You intercept the grab by using a prayer block.*

3H. *Hook his left leg.*

4H. *Complete the move by throwing your attacker backward.*

OPEN HAND ATTACK

1i. *Your attacker is attempting to strike you.*

2i. *As he swings, block with an outside high block.*

3i. *Grabbing his arm, you now strike upward with a palm hand to the chin.*

4i. *You now sweep the leg out with osoto-gari, throwing him down.*

5i. *When you go to the ground you can trap your attacker in a choke hold position.*

BEAR HUG ATTACK

1J. *Your attacker grabs you from behind.*

2J. *As you hold on to him drive your foot straight back to his knee.*

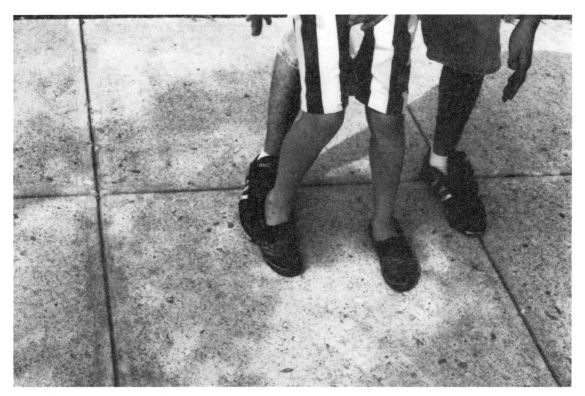

3J. *You then drive your heal to his instep.*

4J. *Complete the move by driving your elbow into your attacker's stomach.*

Combat Blocking Techniques

The following techniques describe some of the basic blocks that you will encounter in your study of self-defense. It is necessary to practice these techniques to build your strength, speed and skill so you can use them effectively in a street situation. There are 20 combat blocks that are taught for various self-defense techniques. You will practice 10 blocks for the right side and 10 blocks for the left side. Remember in most situations without a block there is no self-defense technique. Good luck in your practice of the 20-point combat blocking sequence.

1a. *High block, left side*

1b. *High block, right side*

2a. *Outside middle block, left side*

2b. *Outside middle block, right side*

3a. *Inside middle block, left side*

3b. *Inside middle block, right side*

4a. *low block, left side*

4b. *low block, right side*

5a. *chicken head block, left side*

5b. *chicken head block, right side*

6a. *downward knife hand block, left side*

6b. *downward knife hand block, right side*

7a. *double outside block, left side*

7b. *double outside block, right side*

8a. *outside hook block, left side*

8b. *outside hook block, right side*

9a. *trapping block, left side*

9b. *trapping block, right side*

10a. *double cross block, left side*

10b. *double cross block, right side*

Do's And Don't's of Streetwise Safety for You and Your Child

Educating ourselves as well as our children about the importance of street safety is essential for anyone living in either the city or the suburbs. In the following photos, you will learn the basic Do's and Don'ts of the street and how you and your family can avoid potentially dangerous or even fatal situations.

PARENTS

1. Don't ever leave school with a stranger, even if he or she says that your parents sent them to pick you up, or because they know your name.

2. Don't ever leave your young child unwatched in a recreational area. Form a perimeter with other parents to secure the area.

3. Make sure you always tie your shoelaces when going out. If you have to run you don't want to trip and fall.

4. *Always make sure your child is prepared for school with his lunch and school work.*

5. *Make sure you and your child are familiar with the school teachers. Children become comfortable with school staff they know, especially when trouble arises.*

6. *Children should always know important phone numbers and where to reach their family if they are lost, sick, or just need to tell you where they are.*

7. *Don't talk to strangers who tell you they have lost their animal and want you to help them.*

8. Your child should always have 2 quarters for an emergency call. Stress to them that it is not for bubble gum.

9. Children should always stay as far away from a stranger as they can. Scream for help, and yell, "I don't know this man or woman, please help!"

10. If you are walking with your child always hold his/her hand. Kidnapping is quite a common threat to all children.

11. Stay away from construction equipment, it can be very dangerous.

12. Playing with electrical equipment near any building or construction site can be fatal.

Falling Technique

We all know how important falling techniques can be to protect you if you are knocked to the ground. If a child is pushed forward, backward, or even tackled they need to understand the proper way to hit the ground in order to avoid severe injury. Whether ice skating, rollerblading, running or playing many other sports, if one knows the proper way to land they will be able to walk away from a fall without a bone break or head injury. Let's face it, everyone has taken a fall before. Good luck in your training!

BACK BREAKFALL

1A. *With your feet apart, squat slightly downward with your hands in front of you.*

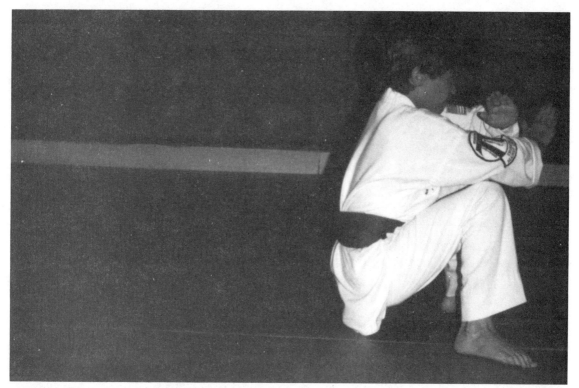

2A. *Now kick your feet out forward and fall backward.*

3A. *As you fall, keep your head up and look between your legs. Keep your arms straight out at your sides so that when you hit the ground they can absorb the shock of your body weight.*

FORWARD BREAKFALL

1B. Step forward with your right foot, preparing to put your right hand on the ground.

2B. Now kick your left leg up toward the ceiling and push off your right foot. Tuck your head down.

3B. *In completing the roll, keep your legs apart so that your knees don't hit each other. You are on your left side with your left hand at your side, and your right hand on your stomach, so there will be no damage to your back.*

AIR ROLL

1C. *As your right hand comes around in a whipping motion, step forward with your right foot.*

2C. *As you swing your right hand down and around, and your left hand down and around, your left leg is whipping straight up toward the ceiling. Your body will now turn in the air.*

3C. *In completing the fall, land on your left side, with your left hand out and your right hand on your stomach, as in the forward breakfall.*

FORWARD FACE FALL

1D. *Place your hands in front of you, your feet about shoulder-length apart.*

2D. *Now kick your feet out from underneath you, with your hands in front, so they are ready for the moment of impact.*

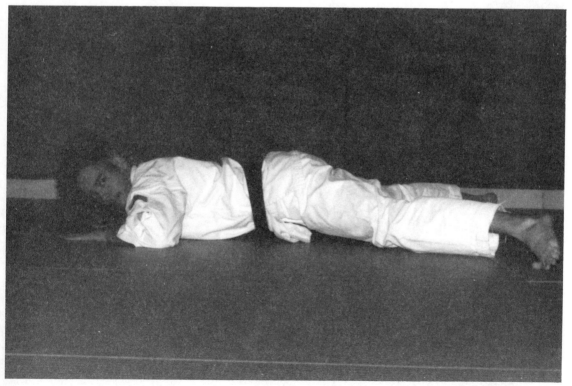

3D. *Turn your head to the left side as your forearms and hands strike the mat. Your body should be suspended in the air with the balls of your feet and your forearms holding you up. Your elbows should not hit the mat.*

Judo Throws

Judo throws for children are good physical conditioning. Young athletes use a lot of strength, technique, and focus in order to perform these movements. Judo is great for body balance and is fun for all children because it promotes a healthy sense of competition.

OSOTO GARI

x1. *Hook up by grabbing your opponent's lapel with your right hand and his/her sleeve with your left.*

x2. *Step with the left foot and pull down on your opponent's sleeve, pushing back on his lapel.*

x3. *Now put your right foot behind your opponent's and prepare to sweep him down.*

x4. *Finish the move by sweeping out your opponent's leg as you hang onto his/her right sleeve.*

OGOSHI

y1. *Stepping with your right foot, grab your opponent's belt from behind.*

γ2. *Now bring the other foot between your opponent's legs and squat down preparing to throw him.*

y3. *Lift him up with your legs and throw him over your head.*

y4. *Complete the move by throwing your opponent to the ground.*

OUCHI GARI

21. *Hook up by grabbing the lapel and the sleeve of your opponent's clothing.*

22. *Hook your right leg behind your opponent's left leg.*

23. *Complete the move by pushing your opponent and sweeping out his/her leg.*

Stances and Hand Strikes

The stances and hand strikes used in practicing your Streetwise Self-Defense are used to develop speed, focus, control and power. It is important to realize that the stances and strikes shown here are being shown from a practice position. When using these strikes on the street you must act quickly.

1. Fighting Stance

2. The elbow strike

3. The reverse punch

4. Open claw hand strike

5. The back fist

6. *The lead knife hand*

7. *Palm hand strike*

8. *Ridge hand strike*

9. *Fingertips claw hand strike*

HAND STRIKES CLOSE-UP

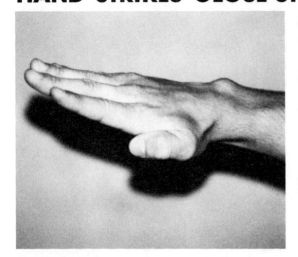

1. Ridge hand

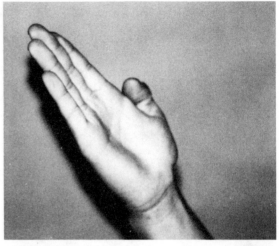

2. Knife hand

3. Palm hand

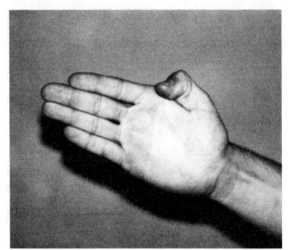

4. Finger tip

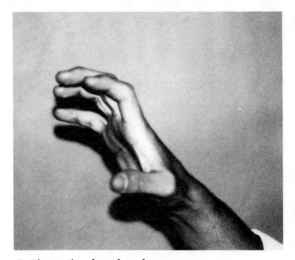

5. Fingertip claw hand

6. Backfist

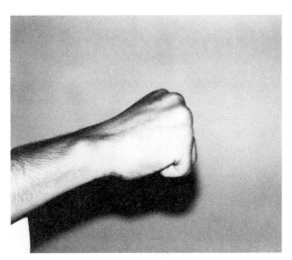

7. Reverse punch

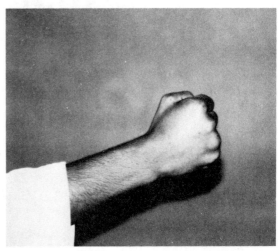

8. Hammer fist

Your Worst Nightmare—Kidnapping!

Make sure your child does not get lured into a kidnapping situation when someone offers them a gift like a stuffed animal or toy. In this sequence of pictures you will see the possible tragedy of a young girl's curiosity. Remember, keep all children in view so this cannot happen, and always educate your child on the Do's and Don't's of safety.

1. The offer to take the stuffed animal as a gift

2. "There's a truckload of stuffed animals in the truck. Come see and take your pick."

3. The comfort zone

4. The grab

5. The forced kidnapping

6. Will you child ever be seen again?

7. Don't think this can't happen to you. Keep an eye on your child!

Note: The license plate is covered and normally the assailant will change vehicles

1A. *Don't walk close to curbs*

2A. *It's quite easy for someone to grab you and pull you into their vehicle.*

Conclusion

I can remember my mother and father telling me to be careful and to look both ways when walking across the street. The threat of getting run over by a passing car or truck was always there. They told me to hold their hands when in the mall or at an event; and to never talk to strangers. We all know the problems children face in this increasingly violent world. Kidnapping, child molestation, and child abuse are spoken about and read about every day in the news.

As an instructor and advocate of anti-crime self-defense programs, I realize the need for all children and parents to educate themselves and become active in forming programs.

Prevention programs for children have become an important necessity in the home, on vacation, in the malls and at all recreational areas. Many incidents, emotional as well as physical, can be avoided if one recognizes the potential danger before it occurs.

Fighting back may not always involve a physical encounter. If it does come down to that, knowing where, what, and how to physically defend yourself is essential. The intention of this book has been to point out different ways of making self-protection easy to remember and comfortable to use.

ABOUT THE AUTHOR AND THE FUMA FEDERATION

A word about the Founder and Executive Director of FUMA; Michael DePasquale, Jr.:

The son of Michael Depasquale, Sr., Grandmaster (Shihan Soke) of the Yoshitsune Waza style of Ju-Jitsu, and one of the founders of Ju-Jitsu in the US, Michael DePasquale, Jr.'s Martial Arts career began in early childhood with Yoshitsune Waza in which he presently holds the coveted rank of Master of the Second Rank (Ni Dai Shihan). During over 30 years of study, practice, competition and teaching in the Martial Arts he has also attained 5th degree Black Belt level in Hakko-Ryu Ju-Jitsu and holds advanced Black Belts in Karate and Judo. A tireless competitor during the 70's and 80's, Michael was honored by Official Karate Magazine as Martial Arts Star of the Year in 1977/78, he won the AAU East Karate Championship in 1981, and qualified for the Pan American Team Trials. His prolonged interest in self-defense has also led Michael to develop his own self-defense style, DePasquale Combat Ju-Jitsu, which has been accepted as a Martial Art in its own right.

In addition, Michael is the Publisher/Editor of Karate International Magazine which he created in 1989 and has appeared on numerous television and radio shows, such as Regis Philbin, Yo MTV Raps, Nickelodeon, Attitudes and the Network News speaking about F.U.M.A.'s Streetwise Safety and Self Defense techniques and seminars.

Michael has also taught the 1st Division Of The Army Special Forces, FBI, U.S. Marshals, Postal Police and many other law enforcement personnel. He has appeared in such movies as "KING OF THE KICK BOXERS," "AMERICAN SHOALIN" AND STARRED IN "CHINA HEAT" PAID IN BLOOD. To date Michael has also been inducted in 6 different Martial Art Halls of Fame. Besides publishing six books with Simon & Shuster, Michael continues to be in demand internationally for his anti-crime self-defense seminars.

You can reach Michael Depasquale Jr. at (201) 573-8028.

THE FEDERATION OF UNITED MARTIAL ARTISTS (FUMA)

Americans have every reason to believe that crime is the leading problem in America today!

According to the FBI's Uniform Crime Report (1), a crime is committed every 2 seconds; every 17 seconds a violent crime is committed, with an aggravated assault every 29 seconds, and a robbery every 46 seconds. Once every 5 minutes a rape occurs and violent crime is increasing rapidly!

The Federation of United Martial Artists (FUMA), a charitable not-for-profit organization registered with the US Internal Revenue Service (2), was founded in 1984 by Michael DePasquale, Jr., internationally known Martial Artist, film star and publisher, to unite Martial Artists in providing law abiding citizens with proactive programs of education and training in crime awareness and self-defense.

As a result of the effort of Michael DePasquale, Jr., since 1984, FUMA membership has grown to include over 1500 leading masters, instructors, students, representing all the Martial Arts as well as concerned citizens who are actively working to make the streets of America safer. FUMA members are engaged in conducting crime awareness and self-defense seminars and training courses, and participating in a variety of other civic activities, throughout the United States and in many foreign countries.

THE FUMA MISSION:

FUMA seeks to focus the enormous positive potential of the Martial Arts world on a single common goal which must certainly be acceptable to everyone: public safety through education.

FUMA fights crime through a proactive approach to personal safety. This approach—aimed at people from all walks of life—features educational opportunities designed to:

- promote awareness.
- develop knowledge and skills for conflict avoidance and resolution and personal protection.
- foster positive personal and civic values and behavior among youth.

WHO ARE FUMA'S CLIENTS?

FUMA has served a wide variety of community service and charitable groups; the handicapped and senior citizens, students in grade school, high school and college, health and law enforcement professionals and military personnel.

HOW DOES FUMA SERVE?

FUMA serves the community through a diversity of activities, examples of which follow:

EDUCATION AND TRAINING

Seminars and Courses:

Seminars on personal protection, home security and corporate crime prevention.

Special proactive personal safety training, tailored to the special needs of groups such as children, senior citizens and the handicapped.

Training in street survival tactics for law enforcement personnel.

Public Information:

Production and distribution of materials on personal safety measures.

Cooperation with local press, government, education and law enforcement in raising awareness.

Self-defense and crime awareness programs on major television programs and networks.
Personal TV and radio appearances by FUMA members.
Newspaper reports on FUMA activities.

COMMUNITY SERVICE

FUMA supports public information programs related to the FUMA mission conducted by government, civic, church or synagogue, law enforcement or commercial groups seeking assistance, e.g., Volunteer Centers, Councils on Aging, the Salvation Army, Rape Crisis Centers, Women's Clubs, and Anti-Drug Campaigns.

FUNDING AND FUTURE PLANS

FUMA's long-range goal is to provide no-cost services to governmental entities, not-for-profit foundations and civic organizations, and to provide minimum-cost assistance to commercial organizations participating in anti-crime activities.

To achieve these goals, we need additional funding to:

- Expand the FUMA funding base to support long-distance travel fees for members to assist civic or charitable organizations which request our support.

- Upgrade FUMA office equipment.

- Support a small part-time staff to better coordinate FUMA activities.

- Support development of additional training and educational materials.

We earnestly solicit financial or material support from corporations, foundations, and all concerned individuals. Material support may include office equipment and supplies or anti-crime educational materials. Please note: All contributions to FUMA are tax-deductible, under Section 170 of the IRS code.

FOR FURTHER INFORMATION ABOUT FUMA MEMBERSHIP, FUMA SERVICES, CONTRIBUTIONS TO FUMA OR TO ARRANGE A STREET-WISE SAFETY AND SELF-DEFENSE SEMINAR FOR YOUR CLUB OR ORGANIZATION PLEASE CONTACT:

MICHAEL DEPASQUALE, JR.
EXECUTIVE DIRECTOR
FEDERATION OF UNITED MARTIAL ARTISTS
P.O. BOX 8585—WOODCLIFF LAKE, NEW JERSEY 07675
201-573-8028
OR
DR. ROBERT C. SUGGS
2507 CULPEPER ROAD—ALEXANDRIA, VIRGINIA 22308